DATE DUE

MAR 2 5 1998		
SEP 1 8 1998		
JUN 1 0 1999		
OCT 1 5 1999		
MAY 1 3 2001		
APR 1 0 2005		

DEMCO 38-296

Kangaroos
& Other Creatures from Down Under

A TIME-LIFE TELEVISION BOOK

Editor: Eleanor Graves
Series Editor: Charles Osborne
Text Editor: Richard Oulahan
    Associate Text Editor: Bonnie Johnson
    Author: Donald Dale Jackson
    Assistant Editor: Peter Ainslie
    Writer: Ann Guerin
    Literary Research: Ellen Schachter
    Text Research: Mary K. Moran Jaroff
    Copy Editor: Robert J. Myer
Picture Editor: Richard O. Pollard
    Picture Research: Judith Greene
    Permissions: Cecilia Waters
Designer: Constance A. Timm
    Art Assistant: Carl Van Brunt
Production Coordinator: Joan Chambers

WILD, WILD WORLD OF ANIMALS

TELEVISION PROGRAM

Producers: Jonathan Donald and Lothar Wolff

This Time-Life Television book is published by Time-Life Films, Inc.

Bruce L. Paisner, *President*

J. Nicoll Durrie, *Vice President*

THE AUTHOR

DONALD DALE JACKSON was born in San Francisco. A staff writer for LIFE magazine from 1963 to 1972, he is the author of *Sagebrush Country* and co-author of *The Sierra Madre* in the TIME-LIFE Books American Wilderness Series. He has also written *Judges,* an examination of the U.S. judiciary through portraits of American judges, and is currently working on a book about the California gold rush. He lives in Newtown, Connecticut.

THE CONSULTANTS

MARY K. EVENSEN received an M.S. in zoology from the University of Minnesota and is presently a research assistant in the Department of Mammalogy at the American Museum of Natural History in New York, specializing in mammalian ecology and evolution. She is currently working toward her Ph.D. in biology at Queens College of the City University of New York.

ROGER F. PASQUIER is the author of *Watching Birds: An Introduction to Ornithology.* He has worked as a curatorial assistant in the Department of Ornithology at the American Museum of Natural History in New York.

SIDNEY HORENSTEIN is on the staff of the Department of Invertebrates, at the American Museum of Natural History, New York, and the Department of Geology and Geography, Hunter College. He has written many articles on natural history and has been a consultant on numerous Time-Life books. He publishes *New York City Notes on Natural History* and is Associate Editor of *Fossils Magazine.*

DR. RICHARD G. ZWEIFEL is Chairman and Curator in the Department of Herpetology of the American Museum of Natural History in New York. His fields of study include the ecology and systematics of reptiles and amphibians, in particular those of America and New Guinea. Dr. Zweifel has published more than 70 scientific papers in addition to semipopular articles for magazines and encyclopedias. His memberships include the American Society of Ichthyologists and Herpetologists, the Herpetologists League, the Society for the Study of Amphibians and Reptiles, the Ecological Society of America and the Society for the Study of Evolution.

Wild, Wild World of Animals

Kangaroos
& Other Creatures from Down Under

Based on the television series
Wild, Wild World of Animals

Published by
TIME-LIFE FILMS

Contents

Introduction

by Donald Dale Jackson

Nothing in this strange country seemed to bear the slightest resemblance to the outside world: it was so primitive, so lacking in greenness, so silent, so old. It was not a measurable man-made antiquity, but an appearance of exhaustion and weariness in the land itself. The very leaves of the trees hung down dejectedly, and they were not so much evergreen as ever-grey, never entirely renewing themselves in the spring, never altogether falling in winter. . . . The smaller birds did not fly away as they did in Europe. The kookaburra approached, uttered its raucous guffaw, then cocked its head, waiting for a response. The kangaroo stood poised and watching. The earth itself had this same air of expectancy, as though it were willing the rain to fall, as though it were waiting for fertilization so that it could come to life again.

—Alan Moorehead, *Cooper's Creek*

Australia is so exotic that it glazes the senses. A palpable air of strangeness seems to cover the land. Nothing looks familiar, yet somehow, paradoxically, everything does. It is not just Moorehead's "ever-grey" eucalyptus trees with their dejected leaves that appear so other-worldly but the very land itself, the barren expanse stretching languidly to the horizon and beyond—"the ghastly blank," explorers called it—and the wildlife, most of all the wildlife, as bizarre and bewildering a menagerie as ever teased a stranger's credulity: an animal with a duck's bill incongruously patched onto a body somewhere between beaver and otter; bats that look like foxes; a wolf with stripes; flying possums; legless lizards; the winsome kangaroo, tall as a man, sheep-faced, twanging across the Outback like some giant grasshopper.

There is nothing else under the Northern Lights or the Southern Cross that is quite like the wildlife of Australia and its immediate neighbors, Tasmania and New Guinea. Why?

To get at an answer one must nudge open the door to the earth's distant past, not a thousand nor even a million years back but 200 and 300 million years ago. It was a time when the oceans and land masses were deployed differently on the earth's surface than they are now and when neither man nor most of the animals we know today had emerged. During that period, scientists believe, there were no continents as they exist now; instead, one gigantic, contiguous land mass covered much of the globe. This supercontinent embraced everything from Greenland to Antarctica, including Australia. Unimpeded by oceans dividing the land, evolving animals moved more easily into new areas of this realm.

The first reptilelike mammals began to appear some 150 million years ago. From this root stock emerged two types of mammals—placentals and marsupials. The difference between them is mainly in their reproductive systems. Placental mammals have a placenta, an organ connecting the body of the mother and her unborn young through which the fetus is supplied in the womb with food and oxygen. Marsupials, lacking such a system, cannot

8   *Dry gullies scar the sands of the Outback in Australia's Northern Territory.*

RAIN FOREST

SCLEROPHYLL FOREST

SAVANNA

SCRUB

DESERT

Timor Sea

Arafura Sea

Darwin

ARNHEM LAND

Gulf of Carpentari

NORTHERN

TERRITORY

Alice Springs

AUSTRALIA

"Red Center"

WESTERN

Indian Ocean

AUSTRALIA

SOUTH AUSTRALI

Great Australian Bight

Adelaide

Perth

protect their young in the womb as long. Born after shorter gestation periods than those of placental mammals, they are less well developed at birth and must survive in an exterior marsupium, or pouch, for many helpless weeks. They therefore compete with placentals at a disadvantage.

In the early stages of mammalian development, marsupials outnumbered placentals, but often when they lived side by side the placentals dominated and eventually shouldered the marsupials aside. (This is not always true. In South America, marsupials and placentals coexist successfully, and in North America the opossum has achieved a *modus vivendi* in a world of placental mammals.)

In time the supercontinent began to break up as earthquakelike upheavals tore a succession of schisms in the land. This vast change isolated wildlife on the several continents that ultimately emerged. Sixty million years ago Australia and Antarctica were still connected but were separated from the other continents. Forty-five million years ago Australia broke off from Antarctica. For reasons that are still unclear, the great majority of animals that had migrated to Australia by that time were marsupial mammals. The more advanced placentals dominated other continents, but in Australia—and only Australia—the marsupials were the dominant mammals.

For the next 15 million years the marsupials were supreme in Australia. They spread throughout the island continent and found their own environmental niches, with no competition from the more intelligent, more prolific placentals; bats and mice were in fact the only placentals in Australia. Then came one final geologic convulsion. This one caused New Guinea to rise from the sea north of Australia. New Guinea became the last and largest in a chain of islands linking Asia and Australia, and along this archipelago traveled various creatures—some of which appear in this book—including snakes, birds, lizards and rodents; the flightless animals probably rafted from island to island on floating vegetation. In time the distance between Australia and the island chain widened, and transportation became impossible for any terrestrial creature lacking wings or oars. When aboriginal man came to Australia from Asia some 30,000 years ago, he came by boat. And with him he probably brought the only large placental

All the Down Under regions mapped and keyed in color at left harbor animals shown in this book. Many species of kangaroos live in the "red center" of the Australian continent, so called for the color of its arid sand and rocks. Sclerophyll forest is characterized by foliage with thickened, hardened leaves that are resistant to water loss.

animal that Europeans found when they landed in Australia in the early 18th century: the dog known as the dingo.

Australia was thus isolated, and its largely marsupial wildlife population was undisturbed and free to develop its own forms at its own pace, to evolve in its own idiosyncratic direction. The shape that the resultant animals took was a product of the two principal determinants of all life forms—the genetic potential of the species and the properties of the environment it inhabits. Australia became a sort of marsupial festival, a laboratory of the lost—"the land of the living fossils," European scientists called it. Whole families of animals that were bumped into extinction on other continents could survive and even flourish in Australia. Perhaps the strangest survivor is the duckbill platypus, which is neither a marsupial nor a placental but an egg-laying monotreme, the most primitive mammal type, most closely related to the reptiles. Monotremes exist nowhere else but in Australia, Tasmania and New Guinea. Platypuses, which feed on stream bottoms, have a smaller brain than other mammals and a venomous spur on their hind legs.

Along with isolation and the opportunities it afforded, the most important factor in shaping Australia's wildlife has been aridity. Most of the Australian landscape is flat and dry—so dry, indeed, that deserts in the continent's center—the grim "Outback"—receive less than five inches of rain a year. Abutting the deserts are vast scrub plains with sparse vegetation and stunted trees. Only on the coastal fringes does the arid character of the country yield. On the tropical northeastern coast are rain forests; dense eucalyptus woodlands grow in the southwest; and forested, well-watered mountains (up to 7,100 feet) dominate the southeastern corner.

Most animals that require a daily drink or a watery habitat live in one of these regions. The others have had to adapt in one way or another to the prevailing aridity. Koalas, whose very name means "no drink" in the language of native Australians, get all the moisture they need from their diet of eucalyptus leaves. Desert-dwelling kangaroo species can go for extended periods without water. There are even wild camels in central Australia, the feral descendants of 19th-century beasts of burden imported from Asia. Most Australian animals have further adapted to the heat and dryness of their homeland by becoming nocturnal, most active during the relatively cool nights.

Obviously, the Australian landscape is not as varied as that of other continents. There are fewer extremes of temperature, rainfall and topography. One consequence of this is that the variety of wildlife is not so great. The species that roam the land represent only several dozen variations on a few basic strains. Kangaroos and possums both derive from a common ancestor that lived a mere 50 million years ago. The "cats" or marsupial carnivores of Australia make up another major category; the long-nosed, insect-eating bandicoots are a third.

Another consequence of the sameness of the Down Under terrain is the domination of a single tree—Moorehead's "ever-grey" eucalpytus. Except in the deserts, the eucalyptuses are everywhere, more than 500 different species, in every size and form. Their special characteristics—their leaves, buds, flowers, logs and their retention of water—are crucial to the life cycles of dozens of animals. The monkeylike cuscus and gliding possums spend their lives in eucalpytuses. Koalas eat nothing but selected leaves of a few varieties of the tree. The numbat, a furry, banded anteater of southwestern Australia,

Morning mist fills a forested valley near Mount Buffalo in the Australian Alps.

12

beds down in dead eucalyptus logs and lives on the termites attracted to the rotting wood.

Exotic, specialized, unique though they may be, the fauna of Australia have a vaguely familiar quality. It is explained by a phenomenon called "convergence." This is the development of similar characteristics, as a response to similar problems, in species not closely related. The marsupial "wolf," for example, has a carnivorous appetite much like that of the North American timber wolf, similar equipment of tooth and fang to satisfy its hunger and a similar body. The chief differences—apart from their reproductive systems—are the striped coat and shorter legs of the marsupial. Though they developed on opposite sides of the earth in sharply different surroundings, the two animals evolved strikingly parallel tools to solve their problems. The final analogy is that both creatures have been pushed to near extinction—and perhaps, in the case of the marsupial, to total extinction—by their biggest problem, two-legged predators.

Marsupial mammals share with their placental cousins the presence of body hair and the ability to nurse their young. There are no important differences in body or muscle structure, though the brain of placental animals is somewhat more advanced. The crucial distinction is in the function of the marsupium in marsupial mammals. Marsupial young gestate for a relatively short period (35 days in the gray kangaroo, 30 in koalas) and when born are invariably insect-sized. A newborn marsupial must navigate blindly on its own across its mother's belly to reach the pouch, crawl in and find a nipple. The pouch harbors and nurtures the developing infant as does the womb of a placental mammal. The time a baby spends in the marsupium varies from 10 weeks for the long-nosed bandicoot to eight months for the red kangaroo. The largest marsupial and the symbol of them all is the kangaroo—"roo" to the Australians. There are actually 47 different kinds of kangaroos and their smaller relatives, called wallabies, ranging from rabbit-sized to man-sized and from the tropical forests to the bare desert of the "red center." The most lovable marsupial is undoubtedly the koala, the bearlike gray-brown tree-climber with the button eyes. Koalas laze away their days in the eucalyptus branches and spend

Terraced cliffs sparsely covered with trees and brush flank placid waters flowing through Dale's Gorge in western Australia.

their nights browsing for the few carefully culled leaves they find tasty and nourishing.

The Tasmanian devil, of exaggeratedly fierce repute, is a heavily built, somewhat piglike scavenger now limited to the large island state of Tasmania. The wombat is another stocky beast, a 60-pound, low-slung grass-eater that lives in deep subterranean burrows. The possum of Down Under is a romantic caped aviator. Five species of possums, known as gliders, have evolved furry membranes that connect their limbs and enable them to glide from tree to tree. Bandicoots are rat-sized rooters that grub for worms in suburban gardens and slash each other with their sharp hind paws. Least attractive, to the minds of many Australians, is the dingo, the placental immigrant that shares its style and reputation with the coyote.

The real dazzle of Australian wildlife is aloft—with the breathtaking variety of glorious and fascinating birds: the bowerbird, which builds an elaborate showcase for himself and even paints its walls to attract his mate; the mallee fowl, which labors for 11 months to create the perfect incubation chamber for its eggs and then deserts them at the moment of hatching; and the ebullient lyrebird, which performs the flashiest song-and-dance act in nature as part of his courtship ritual.

Perhaps because their land is so vast and their population so small, Australians have done comparatively well in maintaining their wildlife. Only six of 123 original marsupial species have disappeared since the coming of the white man. But many have been trapped, harassed and severely reduced in numbers. Koalas were nearly destroyed for their fur two generations ago but are now protected and coming back. No marsupial wolf has been seen in more than a generation. Several of the carnivorous "cats" and bandicoots are considered endangered. Yet many species, including kangaroos, have been granted the sort of protection that now enables endangered animals in the United States to survive, and the roos seem to be flourishing. With the gradual increase in environmental sensitivity, in Australia as elsewhere, it is reasonable to expect that the marvelous laboratory of the lost may be preserved indefinitely.

Close to the center of the continent, the Olgas break up the Outback in a jumble of dome-shaped mountains formed of pebbles, rocks and boulders.

Kangaroos

There is something captivating about kangaroos, something in their gentle manner, perhaps, or their exuberant springiness or maybe just their exotic appearance that makes them appealing. People have always been fascinated by them. When the first live specimen of "the wonderful kanguroo" was exhibited in England in the 1790s, a handbill teased potential spectators by claiming that "to enumerate its extraordinary Qualities would far exceed the common Limits of a Public Notice."

Kangaroos are full of surprises. It is surprising, for example, to learn that kangaroos come in dozens of sizes, from the 180-pound, eight-foot-long red kangaroo of the arid Australian plains to the 16-inch-long rat kangaroo of the tropical rain forest. In between there are kangaroos with dimensions, if not profiles, similar to rabbits, raccoons, fox terriers and sheep. There is a kangaroo, or wallaby—the name applies to the smaller varieties—for every Down Under habitat: rock wallabies that live in broken rocky terrain, big gray kangaroos, or "foresters," that graze in the forest clearings, mountain "euros" of the hill country, reds of the plains and even tree kangaroos, which live a monkeylike life in the branches.

Even more astonishing than their variety is the manner of their birth, incubation and development. A newborn kangaroo is less than an inch long, blind, hairless and weighs less than a gram (about 1/25th of an ounce). It looks like a slimy slug with minute, partly formed appendages. Its equipment consists of instinct, open nostrils with a good sense of smell and forelegs with tiny claws that are just strong enough so that it can crawl from the mother's birth canal, located under her tail, through the thicket of her fur to her pouch, which is on her stomach. This it does during the first and most dangerous three minutes of its life. Once inside the pouch, the uncertainty is over; the baby unerringly finds a nipple and spends the next several months clinging to it tenaciously while its body slowly develops. The pouch is in effect an open womb, where the kangaroo fetus grows and takes shape after birth, in the same way that a placental mammal develops inside its mother's uterus prior to birth.

Young kangaroos spend from three to eight months, depending on the species, developing within the mother's pouch and another four to six weeks as part-time pouch residents, exploring the outside world but continuing to feed in the pouch at mealtimes. To allow the baby, called a "joey," to climb in and out of her pouch, the mother bends down and spreads her forelegs. Even after it has been weaned, a joey continues to stay close to its mother, and it may be as long as a year to 18 months after its birth before it goes bounding off on its own.

Another marvel of kangaroo nature is the mother's ability to hold an embryo in a state of suspended development until the older joey is out of the pouch. A female may mate again within days after giving birth, but when the baby in the pouch is suckling, the second embryo is in a state of arrested development. Its gestation does not continue until the older joey departs the pouch. Sometimes a departed but not yet weaned joey will poke its head into the mother's pouch and nurse along with its newborn sibling at mealtimes for as long as four months. One result of the process—called embryonic diapause—is that a mother kangaroo almost always has a baby in the pouch.

The kangaroo's most obvious talent is its high-jumping and broad-jumping skill. Powerful, muscular thighs and disproportionately long hind feet enable a large kangaroo—the Australians call them "roos"—to cover as much as 27 feet or clear a 10-foot-high fence. A kangaroo can travel up to 40 miles per hour for short distances, but it tires quickly. Females often jettison their older babies when alarmed or pursued. It is not known whether this is a deliberate maneuver to protect the young or the result of blind panic. Kangaroos tend to become panic-stricken when frightened, sometimes bunching up against a fence they could easily clear if they tried. At other times they display apparent boldness, reversing an escape dash and running directly at their pursuers, clearing them in one big leap. Paradoxically, they appear to have no fear of automobiles, and thousands of them are killed annually on the roads of Australia, mainly while foraging at night.

The principal foes of roos—besides leather merchants, sheep ranchers and cars—are dingoes, foxes and eagles. Placid by nature, kangaroos will nevertheless fight when cornered or aroused, jabbing like boxers with their forepaws and lashing out swiftly with their formidable hind feet, which are capable of opening a man's stomach.

The hunting of kangaroos is now banned by all of the Australian states, and the populations are in no present danger of extinction. Estimates of their numbers in Australia range as high as 100 million—seven kangaroos for every human Australian.

Western gray kangaroos

Kangaroos like the western gray at right often spend their entire day resting and grooming in the shade. When no shade can be found, as on the plains of New South Wales, they camp in direct sunlight. In spite of such exposure, kangaroos drink very infrequently, since they get the moisture they need from the vegetation they eat. One group of confined kangaroos that went 70 days without drinking the water their keepers set out for them showed no ill effects.

Stretching for the leaves of a eucalyptus tree, a western gray kangaroo (left) stands on its hind feet and pulls the limb down with its forepaws. Gray kangaroos are strict vegetarians, eating a variety of grasses, bushes and tree leaves. Their teeth are especially suited for grazing, and the stomach resembles those of such ruminants as cows.

Red kangaroos, like the one shown on the run at right, are the most prodigious leapers in the kangaroo family. A pursued red was observed broad-jumping 27 feet in a single stride and clearing a 10-foot-high obstacle. When not under stress, a red kangaroo's stride averages four to five feet; a slight increase in speed may extend the distance to as much as 12 to 14 feet.

The Gregarious Mob

Depending on the weather, a day in the life of the gray kangaroo (left) may be full of activity or drowsy with sleep and indolence. A night feeder in the prevailing hot weather, the gray remains active throughout the day in cool or wet seasons, grazing on grasses or foliage, with frequent breaks for rest and grooming its fur. Kangaroos seek shade whenever it is available and will often return to the same shady spot day after day. One group traveled three miles each day to sit under a certain clump of shade trees.

Kangaroos are gregarious creatures, living together in small social groups and feeding or traveling in much larger ones ranging from 50 to 60 animals to several hundred. Such an aggregation is aptly called a "mob," for it best describes their behavior when alarmed. Warned of danger by a loud thump on the ground from the hind foot of an alert individual, the kangaroos scatter madly in all directions. A few will usually race directly toward the source of danger itself, which they will dodge or attempt to leap over in their frantic urge to escape.

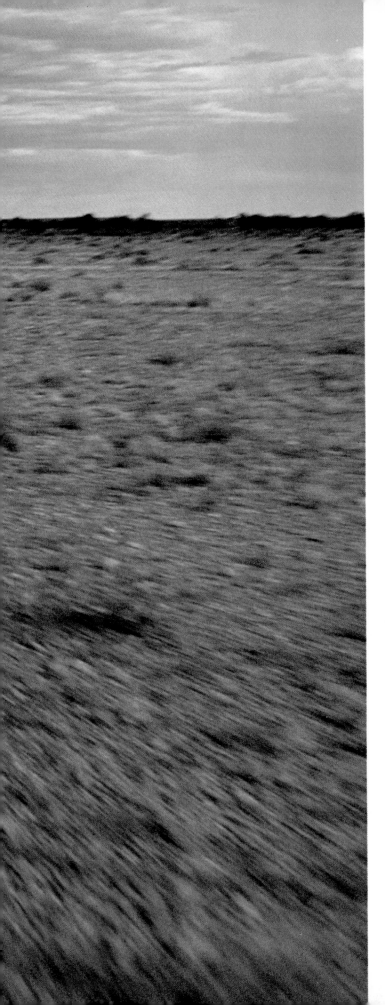

A red kangaroo (left) flees across the scrubland of eastern Australia. Male reds have been clocked for short distances at 35 miles per hour. Young mature females are even faster—capable of brief bursts of 40 miles per hour.

A male red kangaroo paws a female red (above) in what may be a courtship gesture leading to mating. A male, called a boomer, detects a female, or rover, in season by her odor; then he follows her for up to two hours before finally grasping the female's tail, neck and chest in the act of copulation. Males generally produce a soft clucking noise while pursuing females. Though the females are usually silent, they may cough loudly, usually the sound of a disturbed or angry kangaroo, when the males finally corner them.

Mother and Joey

When a newborn kangaroo crawls up its mother's belly and into her pouch, the mother seems completely unconcerned about the baby. But after six months, when the joey begins leaving the pouch and venturing out on the ground, the attachment between mother and offspring grows strong. At first the mother kangaroo allows the joey out for only a few minutes a day, then for progressively longer periods. When it is time for the joey to climb back into the pouch, she makes it easier by spreading her forelegs and bending her body down. The joey, approaching from the front, grasps the pouch opening and tumbles in head first (left), then turns a somersault and positions itself with its head near the entrance.

Around the age of eight months a red kangaroo joey spends most of its time outside the pouch, and another newborn infant takes its place. Still, the joey continues to suckle for four more months before it is completely weaned. In a remarkable adaptation, the mother manages to nourish both offspring properly by producing two kinds of milk at the same time. One, rich in protein and low in fat, supports the rapid growth of the infant attached inside the marsupium to its own nipple. The other, low in protein and rich in fat, supplies the half-weaned joey when it puts its head into the pouch to suckle.

After entering its mother's pouch head first, a gray kangaroo joey peers out of the opening (left). Gray kangaroo joeys use the pouch 310 days before weaning, longer than any other marsupial. In contrast, red kangaroos linger in the pouch around 240 days. Even after weaning, grays continue to stick close to their mothers for as much as six months longer.

A half-weaned gray kangaroo joey, comfortably propped in its mother's pouch (right), grazes with its parent. It is the kangaroo's taste for grass—a staple in its diet—that has stirred the hostility of sheepherders and resulted in the slaughter of thousands of the animals.

Mother and joey gray kangaroos relax together in the midday heat (right). A mother decides when her joey leaves the pouch for good. One female was observed relaxing her pouch muscles when the time came so that the joey tumbled out. Frustrating its attempts to reenter, she grasped it firmly and held it away from her, then hopped off until the youngster got the message.

25

Kangaroo

by D.H. Lawrence

Although he is best known for such novels as Sons and Lovers, Women in Love *and* Lady
Chatterley's Lover, *the British writer D. H. Lawrence began his literary career·in 1909
as a poet. During World War I Lawrence and his German-born wife, Frieda, were forced to
leave England. In their search for a new place to settle, the couple traveled widely and lived
briefly in New South Wales, Australia. Lawrence became fascinated by the extraordinary
plant and animal life of the region, and in 1923 he published a book of verse called* Birds,
Beasts and Flowers *that includes the following poem, "Kangaroo."*

In the northern hemisphere
Life seems to leap at the air, or skim under the wind
Like stags on rocky ground, or pawing horses, or springy scut-tailed rabbits.

Or else rush horizontal to charge at the sky's horizon,
Like bulls or bisons or wild pigs.

Or slip like water slippery towards its ends,
As foxes, stoats, and wolves, and prairie dogs.

Only mice, and moles, and rats, and badgers, and beavers, and perhaps bears
Seem belly-plumbed to the earth's mid-navel.
Or frogs that when they leap come flop, and flop to the centre of the earth.

But the yellow antipodal Kangaroo, when she sits up,
Who can unseat her, like a liquid drop that is heavy, and just touches earth.

The downward drip
The down-urge.
So much denser than cold-blooded frogs.

Delicate mother Kangaroo
Sitting up there rabbit-wise, but huge, plumb-weighted,
And lifting her beautiful slender face, oh! so much more gently and finely lined
 than a rabbit's, or than a hare's,
Lifting her face to nibble at a round white peppermint drop, which she loves,
 sensitive mother Kangaroo.

Her sensitive, long, pure-bred face.
Her full antipodal eyes, so dark,
So big and quiet and remote,
 having watched so many empty dawns in silent Australia.

Her little loose hands, and drooping Victorian shoulders.
And then her great weight below the waist, her vast pale belly
With a thin young yellow little paw hanging out,
    and straggle of a long thin ear, like ribbon,
Like a funny trimming to the middle of her belly,
    thin little dangle of an immature paw, and one thin ear.

Her belly, her big haunches
And, in addition, the great muscular python-stretch of her tail.

There, she shan't have any more peppermint drops.
So she wistfully, sensitively sniffs the air, and then turns, goes off in slow sad leaps

On the long flat skis of her legs,
Steered and propelled by that steel-strong snake of a tail.

Stops again, half turns, inquisitive to look back.
While something stirs quickly in her belly, and a lean little face comes out,
    as from a window,

Peaked and a bit dismayed,
Only to disappear again quickly away from the sight of the world,
    to snuggle down in the warmth,
Leaving the trail of a different paw hanging out.

Still she watches with eternal, cocked wistfulness!
How full her eyes are,
    like the full, fathomless, shining eyes of an Australian black-boy
Who has been lost so many centuries on the margins of existence!

She watches with insatiable wistfulness.
Untold centuries of watching for something to come,
For a new signal from life, in that silent lost land of the South.

Where nothing bites but insects and snakes and the sun, small life.
Where no bull roared, no cow ever lowed, no stag cried, no leopard screeched,
    no lion coughed, no dog barked,
But all was silent save for parrots occasionally, in the haunted blue bush.

Wistfully watching, with wonderful liquid eyes.
And all her weight, all her blood,
    dripping sack-wise down towards the earth's centre,
And the live little-one taking in its paw at the door of her belly.

Leap then, and come down on the line that draws to the earth's deep, heavy centre.

The Lumholtz kangaroo (left), eyes gleaming against the twilight, is as agile in a tree as a monkey. Such tree kangaroos travel rapidly through the forest canopy, leaping as much as 30 feet from one tree to another and as much as 60 feet from tree to ground without injury. Like most marsupials, tree kangaroos, with their superb night vision, are able to navigate confidently in the dark.

One of the smallest of the kangaroo-related marsupials, a long-nosed rat kangaroo (below) stretches to feed on a tea tree bush. Also known as potoroos, from an aboriginal name meaning long-nosed kangaroo, the animals inhabit regions of thick scrub, feeding primarily on insects, vegetation and tubers, which they dig out with the long claws of their forepaws.

Roo's Relatives

Kangaroos and their dozens of relatives are all believed to have descended from small, tree-climbing, ratlike ancestors with prehensile tails. No one knows why these tree-climbers abandoned their arboreal life and developed the shortened forelegs, long hind limbs and counterbalancing tails that are characteristic of today's kangaroos. Even more puzzling is the fact that some of them later returned to the trees. Those that did so gave rise to animals like the Lumholtz kangaroo (above) and the dusky tree kangaroo (opposite), neither animal equipped with the prehensile tail or the grasping paws of its ancestors. In readapting to arboreal life, the tails of both have grown longer, serving now as a supple pendulum or a rigid balancing pole and a means of bracing the animal when climbing. To give them a better grip, their foot pads have grown softer.

The long-nosed rat kangaroo at right is a small land-dwelling member of the family whose size—16 inches long, including a nine-inch tail—approaches ancestral dimensions. Rat kangaroos sometimes use their forepaws to run in a kind of gallop but more frequently bound along on their hind legs in 16-inch leaps.

Wallabies: Acrobats of the Outback

Wallabies are identical to kangaroos in many respects but are commonly distinguished as a separate branch of the family because of their generally smaller size. Even this distinction is somewhat artificial, however, for though some wallabies are no larger than rats, the larger ones are virtually the same size as the smaller kangaroos. The great variation of sizes probably results from evolution in different environments; wallabies have adapted to almost every available habitat in Australia and the nearby islands. Two examples are the medium-size ring-tailed rock wallaby (left), which inhabits the rocky ranges and hill country throughout Australia, and the larger black-gloved wallaby (opposite, below), which lives in the forests and sandy plains of southwestern Australia.

The body size of the ring-tail—around two and a half feet—is almost doubled by the length of the tail, which is bushy and cylindrical and used more as a balancing aid on narrow ledges and steep slopes than, in the manner of other kangaroos, as a prop for sitting. Ring-tails are extraordinary athletes, well adapted for life in the rocky Outback. The hind feet are thickly padded with rough soles to grip rock surfaces that have become polished to a glasslike sheen by the passage of generations of wallabies. Ring-tails are capable of horizontal leaps of up to 12 feet (above) across crevices and between boulders.

A ring-tailed rock wallaby executes an impressive leap and a perfect two-point landing in the series of pictures above. Ring-tails spend their days holed up in crevices and caves, coming out in the cool of the night to graze on the different grasses that make up their diet.

A black-gloved wallaby (left), so named for the black fur on the forepaws and hind feet, feeds on a eucalyptus flower. The soft fur of black-gloves, as well as that of several other wallaby species, is highly valued by Australians and led to the extirpation by fur hunters of the eastern variety of black-gloves.

Overleaf, a group of wallabies, as sociable as their kangaroo relatives, leaps across the grassland bordering an Australian waterway. In the past, the wallabies' diet of grasses marked them as targets for destruction by sheepherders, who have long regarded wallabies as prime competitors with their herds for the grasslands. But governmental conservation laws now protect these lightweight kangaroos in their native savanna.

Koalas

With its soft fur, button eyes, patent-leather nose and general similarity to the toy bear named after Teddy Roosevelt, the koala is plainly irresistible. To look at a koala, for most people, is to feel an overwhelming urge to hold and fondle it. But, beguiling as they are, koalas are still animals and not toys, as Mrs. Eleanor Roosevelt found out when she impulsively picked one up on a visit Down Under and received a painful scratch from the sharp claws of the aggrieved animal.

Despite Mrs. Roosevelt's experience, koalas are almost as amiable as they look. Australians were quick to point out that the former First Lady had lifted the animal the wrong way—by holding it under the arms as one would a child. The correct technique is to face the koala and grasp its forearms, and it will instinctively reach for the lifter.

Koalas, contrary to popular belief, are not bears, though their wooliness and large heads led some early travelers in Australia to call them bears. The misnomer has persisted to the present. In fact they have little in common with bears except their appearance and a somewhat shambling gait. They are vegetarians and tree-dwellers, while bears live largely on the ground and some eat meat. In addition, koalas have a pouch, like other marsupial mammals, and they lack a tail.

"The graveness of their visage," a naval officer wrote in 1802, "would seem to indicate a more than ordinary portion of animal sagacity." Later skeptics suspected that the solemn-looking koala the officer encountered may have been merely sleepy. The name "koala" derives from an aboriginal word meaning "no drink," a reference to the little marsupial's total lack of interest in water. Koalas apparently get all the moisture they require from leaves.

When captured young, koalas will become gentle and affectionate pets. In fact their easygoing amiability came close to being their undoing. They tend to be sluggish and slow-moving, unafraid of man and therefore easy prey for the fur hunters who drove them to the edge of extinction. When a flashlight is beamed on a tree-hugging koala, the lethargic little creature is apt to stare back blankly rather than scurry to a safer haven like other, more wary animals. The combination of their vulnerability and the popularity of their pelts precipitated a slaughter of enormous proportions in the early years of this century. In 1920–21 more than 205,000 koala skins appeared on the Australian fur market. Three years later, over two million pelts were ex-

ported. Some were labeled "wombats" to avoid the hostility of koala fanciers.

Although koalas are no longer found in western Australia, they now enjoy the status of a protected species in the eastern and southern states of New South Wales, Queensland and Victoria. They have been bred, stocked in special reserves and even reintroduced in several areas where they had either declined drastically or vanished altogether. A heartening indication of their comeback is the appearance of road signs in Australia reading "BEWARE OF KOALAS CROSSING ROAD."

When a koala does cross a road, it is only to get to another tree. The animals live their entire lives in trees, and their principal food consists of the mature leaves from certain limited species of eucalyptus trees as well as mistletoe and box leaves. They are among nature's most fastidious eaters. Zookeepers have found that the best tactic for feeding them is to offer a smorgasbord of various eucalyptus leaves and let them shop until they find some they like. Their opposable fingers and sharp claws give them the ability to maneuver on trunks and branches, and they have pouches in their cheeks where fibrous leaves are stored and moistened for easier digestion. They are nocturnal in their habits, spending their days drowsing among the branches and their nights browsing for the two and one half pounds of very special leaves they eat before dawn.

Koala young, like baby kangaroos, must navigate blindly through the maternal fur immediately after they are born to find the pouch where they spend their first six months. The female koala's marsupium is rear-facing, which is awkward for a tree-climbing animal. After a pouch life of six months the pups shift to the mother's shoulders. They reach sexual maturity at three or four years of age, and some have survived as long as 20 years. A full-grown koala weighs about 22 pounds.

Wildlife managers in Australia use a long pole like a cherry picker with a noose at the end to snare koalas in order to move them. They report that the animals remain amazingly calm during this unsettling procedure. When they are released, the koalas have to be shooed up the trunks of their new homes. People who have kept koalas as pets say they seem to be particularly fascinated with mirrors, spending long periods studying their furry reflections, as if they knew—and somehow savored—their own beguiling nature.

Living Teddy Bears

The captivating and comical bundles of silver-gray and white fur shown clinging tenaciously to the branches of a gum tree at right are koalas, the largest of the phalangers and, after the kangaroo, the best known of the Australian marsupials. First spotted in 1798 by a young explorer in the Blue Mountains west of Sydney, the toylike tree dwellers were commonplace and abundant at the time. But forest fires, epidemics and, above all, the guns of fur hunters decimated their ranks. In 1927 alone in Queensland, 10,000 licenses were granted to hunters, and 600,000 koala furs were exported.

Fortunately, steps were taken to prevent the slaughter of the species, and koalas are now making a comeback. But the population increase has been slow because of the koala's low reproductive rate. The koala breeding season is from September to January—spring and summer in Australia—and the gestation period is 25 to 30 days. The single baby, which weighs about two tenths of an ounce at birth, remains in the mother's pouch for six months and is dependent on her for a year. Because koalas feed almost exclusively on the mature leaves of certain eucalyptuses, they smell like eucalyptus cough drops.

A mother koala and her baby (left), perched high in a eucalyptus tree, take their ease. The baby is weaned by munching on half-digested food that has passed through the mother's digestive tract. Gradually, the young koala becomes adjusted to a diet of tough gum-tree leaves rather than mother's milk.

A young cub, fingers clutching its fur, hurtles out of a tree in a leap toward the greener leaves of another tree. Mature koalas are more deliberate when changing trees, usually descending tail first to the ground. Their fastidious tastes make koalas difficult to keep in zoos. They will eat only the properly aged leaves of a narrow range of eucalyptus varieties. Leaves that are too young contain poisons that kill koalas—as more than one rueful zookeeper has discovered.

Phalangers and Wombats

Phalangers, known popularly as "possums," fill the same niches in Australian ecology that are occupied in other latitudes by monkeys, squirrels, sloths and opossums. The Australian possum and the North American opossum, the only marsupial mammal to survive in North America, are in fact distant relatives. Wombats, associated on the evolutionary tree with phalangers, are unique.

Phalangers are densely furred tree-dwelling night creatures of Australia, splendidly adapted for their role. All of them have monkeylike opposable toes that equip them as versatile and confident climbers. The majority of the 44 phalanger species have prehensile tails that they use as monkeys do, as a "fifth paw," to help get from branch to branch when the claws are otherwise engaged. Most phalangers have large eyes to facilitate night vision. A number of them have evolved still another refinement adapted to their life amid the leaves: flaps of skin connecting their limbs and serving as wings that enable them to glide from tree to tree.

Each of the three primary groups of possums—the brushtails, ringtails and pygmies—has evolved its own gliding species. The brushtails, with foxes' faces and pert, prominent ears, have produced the squirrel glider, the fluffy glider and the sugar glider, the most common of the gliders. Ringtails, so called because of the way they loop their long tails, are the evolutionary forebears of the largest gliding phalangers, the three-foot-long greater glider and the yellow-bellied glider. And from the tiny pygmy possum, with its bulging eyes and inquisitive expression, has derived the smallest glider, the feathertail or pygmy glider.

Gliders feed almost exclusively on insects, blossoms, nectar and leaves, although a sugar glider may occasionally splurge on a small bird. These animals glide by extending their limbs full length and stretching the connecting membranes until they resemble small flying carpets. They use their tails as rudders. Their aerial range depends on their size and altitude. The largest can cover as much as 120 yards in the air, while the mouse-sized feathertail sails not much more than a yard at a time. But they only glide and do not truly fly. They will commonly soar from a treetop to the base of another tree, landing with a slight upsweep that enables them to avoid the ground and the predators lurking there. Airborne gliders are said to utter a sound described as a "bubbling shriek" which probably enables the gliders to locate themselves in relation to one another.

Sugar gliders and feathertail gliders bed down together in large colonies, most frequently in a hollowed-out tree where they are safe from most predators except the large climbing lizards. The greater glider is solitary. All young gliders are raised in marsupial pouches, and sugar glider offspring are the most reluctant to leave home, often staying with their parents for two years.

The largest phalanger, weighing about 15 pounds, is an odd-looking furry climber named the cuscus, an animal that seems to provoke harsh reactions for no other reason than its strangeness. "Probably the ugliest of all marsupials," the Encyclopedia Britannica comments.

The cuscus is a slow-moving, bug-eyed creature with ears that are often hidden in its light-colored coat. The upper half of the prehensile tail is covered with fur, while the lower or business half is hairless with a series of traction ridges. The cuscuses are often faulted for their unpleasant musky smell, but it is their telltale odor that aboriginal hunters follow to locate and kill them. Vegetarians that pass their days in hollow tree trunks and are unable to glide like some other members of their family, cuscuses are more common in New Guinea and nearby Pacific islands than in Australia, where their range is limited to the subtropical Cape York Peninsula in the northeast.

The wombat, which may have an ancestral kinship not only with phalangers but also with koalas, is unlike either of them or any other animal. Built stockily and low to the ground, wombats can grow as large as 60 to 80 pounds; they resemble a cross between a badger and a groundhog. Inoffensive vegetarians and burrow dwellers, wombats live in intricately excavated warrens that often have passageways as long as 100 feet.

Some 20,000 years ago there were a number of giant marsupial species, including a bear-sized wombat, but it was probably too mild-mannered to survive. Its descendants dig with their strong claws and munch their grass diet with two rodentlike incisor teeth on each jaw and 20 molars or cheek teeth. Like a koala, a female wombat has a rear-facing pouch that is a distinct advantage for a burrowing animal. If the pouch was front-facing like that of a kangaroo, it would quickly fill up with dirt. Scientists speculate whether a koala might be a wombat that took to the trees a few millennia ago or, conversely, whether a wombat might be a onetime koala that developed an aversion to heights.

Golden possum

Cosmopolitan Possum

Of all the marsupial families in the Down Under region, the phalangers are one of the most widely distributed—particularly on mainland Australia, Tasmania and New Guinea but also eastward to the Bismarck Archipelago and the Solomon Islands and westward to Celebes. Among the phalangers, the brush-tailed possum is one of the most familiar. It is perhaps the only marsupial that has adapted well to changes in its natural habitat, often making its home on top of houses in Australian cities and suburbs.

Although it is primarily a tree-dwelling creature, the brush-tailed possum is also found in treeless, even semidesert areas, living in the caves and burrows excavated by other animals. Brush-tails breed throughout the year; after a gestation period of approximately 17 days a single youngster is born. The young possum stays in its mother's pouch until it is about five months old, then rides around on her back (above) in the manner of North American opossums. During this time the young brush-tail is gradually weaned, becoming totally independent at the age of six months.

A brush-tailed possum (left) perches precariously at the end of a bare tree limb, some 30 feet above the ground. Brush-tails are nocturnal, taking shelter in the hollows of trees during the day. Their natural enemies, other than man, are few—principally monitor lizards and wedge-tailed hawks—which is a big factor in their ability to survive and proliferate.

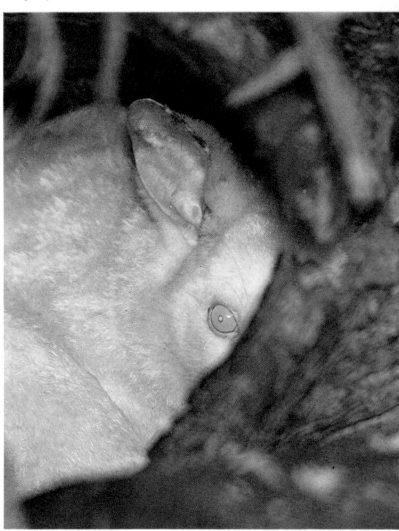

An albino brush-tailed possum tries to retreat to the darkness of a hollow log. Despite its marked differences of coloration, the albino is a true brush-tail and behaves exactly as its normally colored relatives do. The albino's pink eyes, however, lack protective pigmentation and are more sensitive to light.

43

Feeding on a banksia blossom is a messy business for the southwestern pygmy possum shown above. Its soft, silky fur and claw-tipped fingers have become sticky with the flower's nectar. With a minimum body length of only three inches, the pygmy possum is among the smallest of the nongliding phalangers.

A New Guinea cuscus (left) settles into a secure spot among the flowing branches of a tree, anchoring itself with its long, scale-covered, prehensile tail. The large, slow-moving animals relax and rest aloft during the day, coming out at night to forage for fruits, leaves, insects and birds and eggs.

45

Looking like a furry kite, a sugar glider (left) takes off from a tree, watched by a wide-eyed companion. Sugar gliders are capable of soaring 50 yards in one leap during their nocturnal hunting forays and have been seen catching moths in midflight. One of the sugar gliders above is eating a grasshopper, another preferred item in its diet. Very young sugar gliders are carried in their mother's pouch during her feeding leaps. But by the age of two months they are too heavy and are left behind in the nests. By the time they are four months old, they are independent but usually stay with the family group for a considerable time.

Graceful Gliders

Sugar gliders are the alert, squirrel-like possums that have evolved from the brush-tailed possums (preceding pages). Medium-sized animals with soft, ash-gray fur, sugar gliders are distinguished by a dark stripe that runs between their large bulging eyes to the middle of their backs.

Small communities or family groups, like the trio below, are made up of adults and their young from several seasons and take up residence in woodlands and eucalyptus forests. At night gliders leap agilely from tree to tree, gathering buds, nectar and blossoms and pursuing insects and even small birds. During the day they take shelter in leaf nests that they make in tree hollows. A glider gathers the material for the nest by hanging by its hind feet from a branch (overleaf, left). After pulling leaves from the tree with its forefeet it passes them, bucket-brigade style, to the hind feet and finally to the prehensile tail, which coils around the material. When a bunch of leaves has been collected, the glider scurries to its nesting hollow.

Perhaps the most graceful of the gliding possums is the smallest, the pygmy gliding possum (overleaf, right). Known scientifically as *Acrobates pygmaeus*, the diminutive gymnast is only three inches long. In addition to the hair-rimmed gliding membrane that connects its limbs, it has a flattened tail fringed with long hairs that provides yet another gliding plane and inspires the pygmy's other common name—feathertail glider.

Two in the Bush

by Gerald Durrell

As founder of the Jersey Zoological Park in the Channel Islands, Gerald Durrell, along with his wife Jacquie, was commissioned by the BBC to go to Malaya, New Zealand and Australia to film a series of wildlife programs entitled Two in the Bush. *During the filming, Durrell, a prolific author and passionate animal lover, kept a journal of their experiences and observations, later published in a book also called* Two in the Bush. *In the excerpt below, Durrell describes his encounter with great glider possums in Australia, a land he called "the attic of the world."*

Standing in the clearing we shone our lights up at the topmost foliage of some giant eucalyptus trees and suddenly, in our torch beams, four eyes gleamed like gigantic rubies. Moving slowly round to a better vantage point, we saw the animals to which the eyes belonged. They looked, at first sight, like a pair of huge black squirrels with long, smoothly furred tails: they were half in and half out of a hole in the trunk where a great branch had been ripped away and left a hollow. Disturbed by the lights, they moved out of the hollow and made their way along a branch and this enabled us to see them more clearly. They really were only squirrel-like in shape—there the resemblance ended. They had furry, rather leaf-shaped ears, and round, vaguely cat-like faces with little boot-button noses; you could see along the sides of the body a loose flap of skin now, as they were sitting, folded along their ribs in scallops like a curtain. I knew they were Possums of some sort but I could not place them.

'What are they?' I whispered to Bob.

'Greater Glider Possums,' he whispered back. 'They're the largest of the Glider Possums—they're fairly common up here. Wait, and I'll try and make them fly.'

He picked up a stick and approached the trunk of the tree. The Possums watched him with interest. Reaching the base of the tree, Bob hit the trunk a couple of mighty whacks with his branch, and immediately the Possums' air of benevolent interest changed to one of panic. They ran to and fro along their branch, chittering to each other like a couple of spinsters who have found a man under the bed. The fact that they were some seventy feet above Bob and quite safe did not appear to occur to them. Bob belaboured the trunk of the tree and the Possums grew more and more panicky; then one of them—uttering a cat-like mew—launched himself off the branch into the air. As he left the branch he stretched out his arms and legs to their fullest extent and, as the flaps of skin along the side of his body became taut to act as 'wings,' he assumed a sort of shoe-box shape, with a head at one end and his long tail streaming out at the other. Silently banking and weaving with uncanny, glider-like skill, he skimmed over the clearing and came to rest on a tree trunk some eighty feet away, with all the ease of an expertly made paper dart. The other one soon followed him, drifting and banking through the air, and eventually landed on the same tree, only a bit lower down. Once they were reunited they both humped themselves up the trunk and disappeared into the thick foliage at the top of the tree. I had been very impressed by the flight of these lovely creatures, particularly by the distance they had covered, but Bob told me that this was a comparatively short glide: they had been known to cover 120 yards in one glide and in six successive glides to cover 590 yards.

Wombat
Dental Chart

Among marsupials, wombats are a breed apart. Because they have teeth unlike those of any other marsupial, they are classified separately in a family all their own. The dentition of wombats is quite similar to that of rodents. Their two pairs of large incisors, one pair in each jaw, are useful for gnawing through roots and bark. Also like those of rodents, wombat teeth grow continuously from below as they are worn down with use.

The coarse-furred, naked-nosed wombat shown on these pages inhabits the forested and rocky regions of southeastern Australia as well as Tasmania and the Bass Strait islands. A second, silky-furred, hairy-nosed wombat is a denizen of the more arid inland areas of the mainland. Both are strong, swift and skillful burrowers that dig by loosening the soil with their front feet and shoveling it out of the excavation with their hind feet. Wombats are timid creatures that hide inside their burrows during the daylight hours, coming out at night to feast furtively on grasses, roots, bark and fungi.

Bandicoots and Numbats

The names given to the Australian land and its wildlife are full of music, a legacy of the aboriginal people who first beheld the land and its animals. It was they who named the kangaroo and koala, as well as the swamp called billabong, the tree known as koolabah and, most euphonious of all, the snake-killing bird called kookaburra. Bandicoot, the name given to several varieties of squirrel-sized marsupials, sounds very much like these aboriginal coinages. But it is an exception. The name arrived in Australia via India and Ceylon, where it started as "pandi-kokku," an Indian word meaning pig-rat. Bandicoot was the Anglicized name given to the Indian rat, and it was passed along to the similar-looking Australian species.

Bandicoots are a sort of Down Under composite, combining prominent features of several other Australian marsupials. They have the teeth of the flesh-eating Tasmanian devil, the large, strong hind feet of the herbivorous kangaroos and wallabies and a slender pointed snout like those of anteaters. Along with this all-purpose construction goes a predictably omnivorous appetite, ranging from vegetation to insects, worms, mice and even chickens.

Except when mating, bandicoots are solitary animals. Females carefully avoid each other, but males will fight when they come into contact. They attack kangaroo-style, leaping and letting fly with their hind feet. The bandicoot's alleged ability to shed its tail like a lizard led to some confusion among early biologists and a sly accommodation by aborigines. The first specimens seen in England were tailless, so when scientists asked the natives to send them more, the animal they sketched as a reference was devoid of tail. The natives, recognizing the bandicoot by its other features, obligingly produced the desired animals by chopping off their tails.

Bandicoots come in a wide variety of subspecies with such descriptive names as long-nosed, rabbit-eared, barred and pig-footed. Like all marsupials, they are born while still minuscule and undeveloped and spend their first two months in the mother's pouch, permanently suckling on the maternal teat. They live in a variety of habitats, from rain forest to desert, feeding at night and holing up during the day in burrows, pits or hollow logs. Their habit of combing and picking parasites out of their coats inspired the Australian expression "miserable as a bandicoot." The longest fingers on each forepaw also serve as cleaning implements to pluck off dirt from their food. Their principal nemesis is an alien predator, the fox, which was imported from Europe by white men and has seriously cut into the bandicoots' numbers in many parts of the country.

The rabbit-eared bandicoot is one of the island continent's most beautiful animals. Its fur is a silky blue-gray, and its long slender tail is a popular ornament among aborigines, who also relish the meat of the rabbit-eared bandicoot. They hunt their quarry by putting their ears to the ground until they locate the underground burrow, which has a single, spiraled entrance, and then digging down to cut off the animal's path of retreat. The hunters then jump onto the ground behind the bandicoot and force it out of its hole.

Long-nosed bandicoots are widely distributed through eastern Australia—a little too widely to suit the residents of the Sydney suburbs. The animal's habit of digging conical pits in its nocturnal forays for worms and insects has unearthed enough garden shoots and roots to muddy its reputation considerably. Nevertheless, its defenders point out, the long-nose is actually doing gardeners a favor by eliminating destructive insects.

Another handsome, modest-sized marsupial with a taste for insects is the numbat, which finds everything it needs in the wandoo gum forests of southwestern Australia. The 10-inch-long, white-banded numbat appears at dawn, probing and turning over downed logs in its constant quest for termites, which it laps up daily by the thousands. The same wandoo trees that draw the termites provide numbats with their hollow-log homes. Preyed upon by foxes, hawks and eagles, numbats are remarkably docile when captured, neither biting nor scratching but emitting only a faint grunt of protest. Numbats lack pouches, although they are true marsupials, and in consequence the infants must cling to the underside fur of their mother. A mature numbat has 52 teeth, more than any other Australian land mammal, but because of their soft diet the teeth are poorly developed.

The smallest marsupial is the two-and-one-half-inch-long planigale, also an insect-eater, which hides in mud cracks and resembles a tiny mouse with a flattened head that is more characteristic of reptiles than mammals. A planigale can eat its own weight in grasshoppers or crickets, some of them nearly as large as the planigale itself. The tiny creatures breed in summer, and, despite their diminutive size, planigale mothers can accommodate as many as 12 babies in their pouches.

Nosy Insectivores

The numbat, or banded anteater, shown at left is widely considered the most beautiful of all the marsupials. Ranging in overall color from a grayish to a reddish brown, with several distinct white bands across its back, the numbat is slightly larger than a rat, not including its bushy seven-inch tail. A dark stripe through each of its eyes accentuates the sharp, pointed shape of its face.

The numbat has a long, sticky tongue that it can extend for several inches, facilitating the capture of its favorite food—ants and termites, which are licked up from the surfaces of fallen sticks and logs. The numbat can be seen on its solitary rounds during the day, a habit that sets it apart from many other marsupials such as the long-nosed and short-nosed bandicoots (below and opposite, below, respectively), which are primarily nocturnal. Because their hind legs are longer than their forelimbs, bandicoots are sometimes mistaken for miniature kangaroos. But their hind legs are not as elongated as those of kangaroos. Bandicoots generally move not by hopping but with a galloping gait, using all four feet as they forage for insects through the open plains, thick scrub, swamp and forests of Australia, Tasmania and New Guinea.

A numbat (above) pokes through debris on the forest floor in search of termites. Since the numbat has difficulty breaking through the rock-hard exterior of termite mounds, it looks for the "white ants" outside the mounds in the rotten logs where they feed.

All bandicoots have pointed snouts, but the short-nosed bandicoot (opposite) has a relatively broader head and wider jaws. Bandicoots are solitary, peaceful creatures, but when two males meet they may fight—and inflict serious injuries with their sharp claws.

A small family of long-nosed bandicoots (right) searches for the insects that make up most of their diet, which they supplement with worms, snails, lizards, mice and plants. Young bandicoots may leave their mother's pouch 55 days after birth. This is a comparatively brief pouch life for a marsupial, particularly one of such small size—only a maximum of 23 inches from head to tail.

Marsupial Carnivores

They are called "cats." But the flesh-eating marsupial animals of the families Dasyuridae and Thylacinidae lumped together under that familiar one-syllable name bear very little resemblance to actual felines. In fact, they bear scant resemblance to one another. One of the Australian "cats" looks like a striped wolf, another could pass as a polka-dotted weasel, a third resembles a wharf rat with a thick brush of a tail. The oddest of them all is the one called the Tasmanian devil, which got its name from its strength, its deceptively fierce expression and its harsh and oddly threatening cough. The figure the devil presents to the world is vaguely reminiscent of a half-dozen other beasts, including a badger, a peccary of the American Southwest and an overweight English bulldog.

Although most of these diverse creatures are carnivorous and thus equipped with the fangs and claws of hunters, at least one dasyurid is an anteater. The only real common denominator among the marsupial cats is the fact that all of them, to one degree or another, have declined to the point of rarity. Some are crouched on the rim of extinction.

The animal known variously as the marsupial wolf, Tasmanian tiger or hyena is the closest to extirpation and may in fact already have disappeared. The last time anybody shot one of the handsome, tiger-striped hunters was in 1930 in its native Tasmania; the last captive specimen died in 1933 in the Hobart Zoo in Tasmania. Since then the only evidence of their existence has been the occasional discovery of a track in the dense rain forests of the island state. Before the settlement of Australia they were common on the mainland, but their ecological role was probably usurped by the more aggressive dingo (pages 76–79), a late arrival in Australia. Sheep ranchers and poultry farmers, angered by wolves' poaching, almost decimated them in the early 1900s, and by the time they became a protected species it was probably too late to save them from eventual extinction. But most evidence indicates that a few survivors probably live on in remote corners of Tasmania.

Known scientifically as *Thylacinus cynocephalus*, the wolves are the largest carnivorous marsupial mammals. Their physical resemblance to the placental timber wolf of North America illustrates the theory of convergence, the similarity of two unrelated species as a result of being confronted with similar problems of survival. The chief differences between the two are the shorter legs of the marsupial wolf and the stripes on its back and tail. The timber wolf is faster, while its marsupial cousin relies more on persistence and endurance to stalk prey.

A distant relative of the wolf, the Tasmanian devil is thickly built and slow, with jaws strong enough to crush the bones of the small mammals and birds that comprise its diet. The devils disappeared from mainland Australia at approximately the same time as the wolves, but have not been slaughtered in comparable numbers in Tasmania, and the surviving devils live on protected reserves. The devil is a ground dweller and only a fair climber. Its litters average three or four kits. The young spend three and a half months in the marsupium, then leave the pouch and cling to the mother's fur until they are weaned at the age of five months. The part of the brain associated with the sense of smell is enlarged in the Tasmanian devil, which suggests that its strongest survival tool may be its nose. Despite its name, brutish looks and reputation for ferocity, the animal can be tamed while young and makes a tolerable pet.

The tiger cat, a speckled tree dweller, has the reputation of being the most combative resident of the Australian bush. Adult tiger cats reach a length of four feet, including their spotted tails, and bear some resemblance to the weasels and martens of North America. They are red-brown in color, extremely wary and muscular, with strong pads adapted for climbing and springing to snatch an airborne bird. The only weakness tiger cats display is a reckless inclination to return to the scene of their crimes, such as chicken coops, and expose themselves to retribution.

The so-called native cat is closely related to the tiger cat but is smaller and more placid; its spots stop short of the tail. Like most other marsupial cats it is nocturnal, preying on birds, insects and small rodents. Scientists say that its numbers have declined seriously in recent decades. One curious aspect of native cat biology is that a female may bear as many as 24 young—through a process called superfetation—but has teats for only eight, thus assuring that only the strongest of the litter will survive.

The tuan looks more like a rat than a cat, but it shares a taste for meat with the larger cats. A rarely seen forest dweller with a nine-inch-long body and a brushlike, eight-inch tail, the tuan has a predilection for stealing miscellaneous items for nest furniture. Australians tell the story of two lumbermen who once got into a violent argument over a pound note that had disappeared. Later, after felling a tree, they found the bill in a tuan's nest.

Tiger cat

Native Cats

When the earliest English settlers arrived in Australia, they got their first look at a new family of animals—the dasyurids, small graceful creatures that ranged in size from the dimensions of a mouse to those of a Springer spaniel. One of them, shown on these pages, was about the size of a domestic cat—18 inches long, with a 12-inch tail. It was promptly dubbed "native cat," although it looked more like a marten with white spots and was not even remotely related to either marten or tabby. Like most dasyurids, the native cats are carnivores and, like most Australian fauna, they are marsupials, although the pouch of the female is no more than a shallow, crescent-shaped pocket that becomes prominent only during the mating season. Although only eight out of every large litter can be accommodated by their mother's eight available nipples, those survivors develop quickly, opening their eyes at the age of two months and going their independent ways two months later.

Like most of their kin, native cats are nocturnal and rarely venture out during the day, as in the unusual photographs above and at right. Like true domestic cats, they tend to settle close to man. They were once abundant in the populous southeastern corner of continental Australia until they were nearly wiped out by a virus in 1902–3. The epidemic compounded widespread slaughter by chicken farmers bent on retaliation for the cats' raids on their coops. The cats have disappeared from most of Australia. There are a few remnant colonies in suburban Sydney, Melbourne and Hobart and in the north and west of Australia, where they live in stone dens and hollow logs.

The Devils of Tasmania

Its name and its satanic reputation, according to many scientists and zookeepers, are undeserved. The so-called Tasmanian devil is more often than not a docile, even affectionate creature, although certain individuals may have vicious natures that have given the animal its bad name. The squat, three-foot-long devils do have an undeniably fierce-looking appearance, especially when they bare their formidable teeth.

Strong, superbly muscled marsupials, the devils once roamed the Australian mainland but disappeared there before the arrival of European colonists. Their exterminator was almost certainly the migrant dingo. On Tasmania, where no dingoes live, devils are still abundant. Carnivores and scavengers, they consume every part of their prey, including fur, feathers and bones, which their powerful teeth crush with ease. They are not finicky in their appetites and will greedily devour carrion or almost any living creature, including sheep, poultry, fish and even the deadly tiger snake, which Tasmanian devils kill with the skill and aplomb of a mongoose attacking a cobra.

A Tasmanian devil cautiously emerges from the water under cover of shoreline foliage (below). Devils frequently use water as a means of escape from enemies, though their usual habitat is in thickets or brush. They are able to climb, but, unlike most of their Down Under "cat" cousins, they usually avoid the trees.

A young Tasmanian devil and its mother survey a water hole. Tasmanian devils take to the water readily, and, although normally nocturnal, they like to bask in the sun after a swim. The three or four babies in each litter remain in their mother's marsupium for three and one half months, and during most of that time the pouch is completely closed, like a zippered change purse—which may be a waterproofing device to permit the mother to swim without drowning her young.

Snarling fiercely and baring its needle-sharp teeth, a crested-tailed marsupial "rat" (above) looks every bit as dangerous as does its larger kin, the Tasmanian devil—and is, in the context of its miniature world. Pouncing on the mice, lizards and small birds that are its principal food, it strikes with lethal speed and dispatches its victims with a single bite on the nape of the neck.

The alert-looking mother and her six scared, half-grown babies (right) are red-cheeked dunnarts, one of 10 closely related species of pouched "mice" that inhabit all sorts of Australian environments, from Outback deserts to humid rain forests. Despite their gentle appearance, they are ferocious predators. They will fearlessly attack small vertebrates, and they can capture highly mobile insects nearly as large as themselves—as demonstrated by the common dunnart shown opposite devouring a grasshopper.

Mixed Mouse Club

The orders of Australian mammals include a sizable group of small marsupials that look remarkably like mice and rats and another host of native mice that are true placental rodents, closely related to common house mice. The pouched "mice" are mostly carnivorous and are, ounce for ounce, as sturdily built and aggressive as their close cousins, the larger marsupial "cats," "wolves" and Tasmanian devils. The native mice are herbivores or insectivores and are generally more timorous and gentler than their pouched imitators.

Some of the marsupial pseudomice occupy the same habitats as placental mice, and at least two of them (overleaf) have even gone so far as to share the same burrows. Along with its indigenous menagerie of mice and their marsupial imitators, the island continent has inevitably become host to those ubiquitous stowaways and universal pests—the common mice and rats of Europe and Asia, which have now become as numerous and firmly established Down Under as they are in every other part of the world where white men have settled.

Pseudomice

The taxonomical identification of Australia's native mice and marsupial lookalikes can be confusing. The tiny creatures at right and below look remarkably alike and occupy the same habitats and often the same underground warrens, yet are distinctly different animals. The Australian hopping mouse, or kangaroo mouse, at right is a placental murid, a vegetarian rodent that is closely related to the familiar kitchen-variety mouse. In Australia kangaroo mice are often mistaken for the jerboa marsupials (below), tiny carnivores that frequently live in the same burrows with kangaroo mice. Jerboa marsupials, unique to Australia, are not to be confused with true jerboas, placental mice of Asia and Africa. The two animals are totally unrelated, although they resemble each other and hop around in the same kangaroo fashion on their long hind legs.

The gentle vegetarian opposite is a member of the genus *Pseudomys*, which is comprised of 10 species of placental Australian mice. With its velvety blue-gray coat, it is one of the most beautiful of all rodents.

Climbing spryly around in spinifex grass, Pseudomys (right) is an adaptable little mouse that lives in many environments of central, eastern and southwestern Australia and Tasmania. It forages during the night and rests in a shallow burrow during the day. When aroused, it moves sluggishly and is easily captured.

The kangaroo mouse (left) and the jerboa marsupial (below) have large ears, very long tails and long, narrow hind legs on which, when they are in a hurry, they hop gracefully in pursuit of food or to escape pursuers. When they slow down, both creatures move quadrupedally in an awkward, ambling gait. Their communal burrows are dug in sandy hills near clumps of grass that serve as convenient hiding places.

Bats

Bat Cleft is the name of a deep cave in a limestone hill near the town of Rockhampton, Queensland. The cave was named for its spring and summer residents—200,000 insect-eating bats of a species known as bent-winged.

The bats begin to arrive at the cave in November, late in the Australian spring. They come in swarms of thousands, their radarlike steering mechanism guiding them to the long crack in the limestone that leads to the cave. They mass on the walls, hanging upside down and dormant during the day. They have wintered in scattered camps—as their congregations are called—in the vicinity. In winter their metabolism slows, they breathe less frequently and their pulse rate is down, allowing them to conserve energy as they lapse into a state of dormancy similar to hibernation. But with the spring warmth their metabolism speeds up and the bats emerge from their torpor. The presence of 200,000 warm bat bodies lifts the temperature of Bat Cleft from 71° to 88° F. within three weeks of their arrival.

Every one of the occupants of Bat Cleft is a female, and every one is pregnant. The males are scattered through the nearby forests alone and in small groups. Having mated with the females during the previous fall, they have completed their job in perpetuating their species. By early December, when the temperature and humidity are right, the young are born—one baby to each mother, pink and blind. The cave, warmed by the thousands of clustered bats, is the infants' incubator.

With the coming of dusk and emergence of night insects, there are signs of restlessness in the cave. A few of the mother bats begin to fly in anxious circles inside the cave. A more adventurous one darts outside to see if it is dark enough. With full darkness the entire adult colony flies from the cave in a solid black column, their pointed ears erect and their beady eyes flashing red in the darkness. It takes an hour or more for the entire colony to leave. The young are left behind, a pink murmuring mass, clinging to the walls. Once in a while a tiny bat loses its grip and falls to the floor, where it is instantly devoured by swarms of brown beetles.

The bats maneuver easily through the forest. They can fly as well as if not better than most nocturnal birds. They buzz the branches in their thousands, each one devouring hundreds of insects during the night's hunt, scooping them out of the air and off leaves and branches.

Like most forest creatures, however, the bent-winged bats are not only predators but prey. Carpet pythons, large constricting snakes that spend their days in rocks around the cave, wait to pick off the smaller bats as they run the gauntlet through the narrow cleft, catching them in their jaws. Big, pale-winged bats called "ghost bats," the only cannibalistic Australian species, swoop out from their nearby retreats and snatch up a few more.

Swiftly the bent-winged bats finish their night's hunt. Before the first light of dawn they start back to the cave. The noise of a hundred thousand wings again fills the stone cavern, turning it into an echo chamber. The young bats immediately begin squeaking for food. Each mother finds its own, and the babies suckle at nipples located where the bats' two-inch-long forearms join their bodies. By the end of December the young have developed fur, and six weeks later they are full-grown and independent. The additional heat generated by the young bats raises the cave temperature to 100° F. By March all but about a thousand of the bats have gone from Bat Cleft to slumber through the coming winter months.

Bent-winged bats, which range as far west as Madagascar, are only one of about 50 bat species found in Australia, a troupe of night fliers that includes the relatively handsome "flying foxes" and the mastiff bat, with a face as wrinkled and pinched as a prune. The largest are the flying foxes, or fruit bats, one of which so alarmed a sailor with Captain James Cook's exploring party in 1769 that the man reported he had seen the devil, horned and winged and "as large as a one-gallon keg and very like it." The faces of the flying foxes are indeed remarkably foxlike, but the bats are unrelated to true foxes.

The wingspan of most flying foxes is between two and four feet, though a giant species in New Guinea with a wingtip-to-wingtip spread of five feet six inches has been reported. Like bent-winged bats, they live in large, sexually segregated camps, numbering up to 500,000 individuals, from which they patrol an area perhaps 20 miles across for their nightly sustenance of blossoms, flowers, nectar and fruit. Scientists believe they are intelligent, citing their ability to learn from unsettling experiences and the fact that some members of each colony serve as scouts in their foraging missions. Aborigines hunt them by lighting fires under their daytime perches, which stupefies the bats, and then knocking them off with sticks and boomerangs. The "bat pie" the aborigines cook is said to be rather tasty.

Reddish fruit bats

Night Fliers

Carolus Linnaeus, the founder of modern animal classification, gave the common rabbit-eared creature above a bad name 200 years ago when he mistakenly accused it of being a vampire. But the giant false vampire bat, or ghost bat, does not suck human blood and should not be confused with true vampire bats, the razor-toothed night fliers of the West Indies and Latin America that are known to attack sleeping humans. Nevertheless, the ghost—one of Australia's largest species, with a wingspan that exceeds two feet—is a cannibal. Among its principal prey are bent-winged bats and other small members of the family, which it catches on the wing during their nightly mass flights.

Most of the 50 species of bats in Australia and Tasmania, however, are fruit eaters or insectivores and harmless to man and other bats. The two-inch Queensland blossom bat, in its customary upside-down resting position at right, prefers nectar and flowers but is also partial to the juices of mangoes, figs and other tropical fruits.

Flying Foxes and Drifting Sand

by Francis Ratcliffe

Of more than 50 species of bats found in Australia, the fruit bats, popularly called flying foxes, are among the largest. Usually content with fruits and blossoms that they find growing in the wild, fruit bats nevertheless began invading cultivated orchards during the period between the World Wars, causing great damage to the crops and huge financial losses to the growers. The Australian government commissioned the respected scientist and writer Francis Ratcliffe to find a way to stop their encroachments. His study produced not only Ratcliffe's official report but also a popular book, published in 1938, entitled Flying Foxes and Drifting Sand, *from which the following is excerpted.*

On the top of Tamborine Mountain there is a settlement of fruit growers mostly. Their land is planted with oranges, bananas, and passion-fruit vines. Bordering the cultivations on all sides rises the wall of the uncleared jungle. . . .

When the night is very dark and very still one's senses seem to grope almost desperately for something to record. I peered and listened until my eyes and ears seemed to strain away from my head. I heard a few soft movements in the forest, and once the long coughing grunt of a possum. From some farm below the mountain came the sound of cattle, and the howl of a dog, so faint as to be hardly audible. Then utter silence. I happened to look up to the strip of sky, and was just in time to see a big shadow glide out of sight behind the trees. I thought it was an owl. Another passed over, soundlessly. A moment later there was a flutter and a rustle in the branches, and then a queer throaty screech which I knew at once was not the cry of any bird. It was a flying fox.

Chance had set the stage rather cunningly: the narrow crack in the dark forest; the silence and expectancy; then the sudden passing of that noiseless gliding shadow. I felt excited, and mine was not wholly the cool excitement of a scientist. There was something in it deeper and more disquieting. I was to experience the feeling not infrequently during my years of association with these creatures. More than once, after hours perhaps of searching and watching in some patch of rain-forest or swamp, I have had to fight back an uneasy desire for sunlight and human company; for the imagination has a knack of jumping the rails when faced for long with the gloom of the jungle or the extravagant weirdness of the mangroves.

For a quarter of an hour or more I watched the foxes passing overhead. They came singly, or in little groups, flying steadily and easily. At times I could hear the sound of their wing-beats, like a whistled whisper. Occasionally one would swoop down to the level of the tree-tops, swinging right and left through the branches. Although they flew like birds, there was nothing birdlike about their pointed wings: the sharp triangular silhouette was unmistakably bat.

The next day I was taken to see the camp by the wife of one of the settlers on the mountain, who brought her eighteen-months-old son with her because he could not be left at home alone. She led the way down the hillside, carrying him in her arms. First the track, which was steep and narrow, passed between banks of luxuriant lantana: then it plunged into the jungle. Presently we came to a grove of palms, and scattered among them were a few big trees, mostly figs and carribins. The figs were grand specimens; the carribins had the bases of their trunks fashioned into a series of radiating buttresses, some of which projected outwards nearly twenty feet. My guide stopped and looked round.

"This is where the foxes used to be," she said, and pointed to the rocks and the dead palm-leaves which were spotted with their dry dung. They probably aren't far off now . . . Ah! There they are."

"Where?" I asked.

"Didn't you hear them?"

"No."

That I did not hear them is quite understandable, for I do not usually hear things, not even the song of birds, unless I consciously stop and listen. Nevertheless I find it hard to realize that for some moments I stood within earshot of a mob of flying foxes and heard nothing. I could not possibly do so now. I quickly learned that the only way to track down the animals, whether in their daytime camps or feeding at night, was by sound. Very soon my ear became extraordinarily sensitive, though to all other sounds but the cry of a flying fox it remained as dull as ever. Before many months had passed the screech of a fox, however faint, would jerk me to attention, whatever I might happen to be doing at the moment.

The new camp was scarcely a hundred yards off, and presently the sound of our footsteps in the dry palm-leaves roused the animals. There was no mistaking the sound now. Their voices, chattering and querulous, blended into one continuous, high-toned murmur. We were among them before we realized it. I was watching the fronds of a palm some distance away, which seemed to be in a state of unnatural agitation, when I discovered that we were the focus of hundreds of pairs of little bright eyes. We were standing under a gigantic fig-tree; its branches were loaded with foxes, hanging head downwards wrapped in their wings. All round us the din was kept up, but the beasts in our immediate neighborhood seemed too curious to make a fuss.

For some time there was hardly a movement, and then the spell was broken. Apparently the foxes decided that we were not worth worrying about (they were soon to learn their mistake, for I carried a gun) and the camp returned to its normal activities. These seemed to consist of fighting, love-making, and scratching themselves with a foot or a wing, though many just bent their heads on their breasts and went to sleep.

Dingoes

In the American West an unsavory but cunning character is frequently described as a "lowdown coyote." The Australian equivalent of the North American wild dog is a "dingo," and when one Australian calls another a dingo, it is the ultimate put-down. Australian dingoes share with American coyotes a reputation for deviousness (and for an insatiable appetite for lambs and calves), a finely tuned set of sensory organs and the implacable enmity of humans who share their habitat. But the most striking parallel between the coyote and dingo is a talent for survival. Both have been attacked with guns, poisons, traps and the miscellaneous weaponry of two continents for more than a century, and both have managed to thrive. Their most dedicated foes are sheep and cattle ranchers. Despite bounties paid for their pelts, they have endured. Their grit and guile have made them campfire legends. In Australia the story is told of a dingo, "Hoppy-Go-Three," who earned his name by chewing off one paw to escape a steel trap. Hoppy watched where he put his remaining feet from then on and even learned to scorn poisoned bait. He continued to feast regularly on lamb, however, but stayed out of range of bounty-hunting "doggers" for so long that they eventually came to admire him. The man who finally shot him, several years after he was crippled, confessed that he felt "kind of sorry" about it.

Dingoes are not native to Australia, but the precise date and method of their arrival are uncertain. The most popular theory is that they accompanied the aborigines, perhaps as camp animals, when these people arrived in Australia from Asia about 20,000 or 30,000 years ago. The oldest known dingo fossil dates back no farther than 3,000 years, which makes it difficult to trace the family tree. Many scientists theorize that the dingo's ancestors were most likely the plains wolves of India made famous in the *Jungle Books* of Rudyard Kipling. A minority view holds that dingoes crossed to Australia on their own when there was still a land bridge to Asia.

Dingoes are about the size of a collie and differ from domestic dogs in their pointed, permanently erect ears and oversized teeth. They are usually tawny yellow with a pale underside and white markings on tail and toes, but some have reddish-brown coats and others are even darker. They go hunting either in the daytime or under cover of night, depending on how close they are to the pressures of civilization. Their habitat includes both forests and the vast treeless plains of central Australia. There is some reason to believe that dingoes follow ancient trails across the continent, moving to the east coast in the winter and back to the west in summer.

Besides domestic sheep and calves, dingoes hunt kangaroos, wallabies, bandicoots, ground-dwelling birds and almost anything else they can catch. Rabbits, which quickly spread through Australia after their introduction from Europe, have become a staple of the dingo diet. A kangaroo pursued by a pack of dingoes will sometimes flee to a water hole, where it will try to grapple with them one by one and drown them.

Male dingoes are territorial, marking the frontiers of their home ground with urine as other members of the dog family do. The young are born in a den, which might be a hollow log, a former rabbit burrow or a rock shelter. Litters average about five pups, but as many as 16 have been reported. The young stay with their parents for a year and sometimes longer, learning to hunt and to avoid their only natural enemies, wedge-tailed eagles and pythons. They hunt silently—alone, in pairs or in small packs. But their silence persists only as long as the hunt. Like coyotes, dingoes like to howl; they do not bark but rather yelp, growl or wail. And, again like coyotes, the sound they make is strangely unnerving. "It's a sound which seems to take you back in one rather breathless moment," wrote a naturalist, "to the days of man the hunter."

Generations of dingoes have been domesticated by aborigines. They are apparently faithful pets, but there is always the possibility that they will "go bush," or return to the wild. Animal collector Joseph Delmont once took a bottle-bred, domesticated dingo with him on a kangaroo-hunting trip in northern Australia. They were awakened by howling wild dingoes, and Delmont quickly leashed his pet. He vividly describes what happened next:

"The animal stood there with bristling flanks. Its eyes dimmed, and a whining sound issued from its throat. From that moment on, the dingo was a changed creature. It ceased to play, ate little, and did not seem to recognize me. One night, when the howl of the dingoes rang out again, I released him, and he bounded off into the darkness. . . .

"Next morning we found his collar surrounded by blood and scraps of skin. He had paid the supreme penalty for his yearning to see his brothers and sisters: they had torn him to pieces and devoured him."

The Dogs of Australia

Dingoes are Australia's largest land predators, standing two feet high and weighing an average of 35 pounds. Once thought to be indigenous wild dogs, dingoes are now considered feral animals, canines that were once domesticated but have returned to their wild state.

The Australian aborigines, who probably first domesticated the dogs, still have a great fondness for them and keep them as pets and hunting animals. To most white Australians, however, they are at best pests and at worst scourges on their cattle and sheep. In addition to poison, traps and other conventional means of pest elimination, farmers have even constructed a 6,000-mile-long, six-foot-high wire dingo fence winding through the states of South Australia, New South Wales and Queensland in the hope of containing the dogs within the arid, uncultivated interior of the continent. To supplement this supposedly dogproof barrier, which is three times the length of the Great Wall of China, some state governments have hired dingo hunters called doggers who receive bounties of $10 for each animal killed. After years of experience with the dogs, even the doggers have developed a begrudging respect for the dingoes' cunning and resourcefulness.

A lone dingo (right) prowls around rocky caves and crevices looking for prey, its tawny coat of dense hair blending with the sandy hues of the parched terrain. Although they are most often solitary predators, dingoes may hunt in pairs or groups. The duo below is stalking a spiny echidna, which makes a futile attempt at hiding under a rock.

Platypuses and Echidnas

The duckbill platypus is an Australian original. It exists nowhere else in the world, it looks and acts like nothing else, and in fact there was a time when it wasn't *believed* anywhere else. Skeptical English scientists, on first seeing a preserved specimen, were convinced that it was a joke—parts of several animals sewn together by devious taxidermists. It isn't hard to see why they reacted that way. The animal's face suggests a cartoon duck, an otherwise furry creature with its nose seemingly stuck in a leather glove. Beady eyes peer above the rim of the flexible, acutely sensitive bill, and above them are dark slits, the only visible parts of the ears.

The 19th-century scientists suspected that the platypus was another creation in the tradition of the notorious "eastern mermaid," which artful Chinese had constructed from a monkey's topside stitched to a fishtail and sold to gullible sailors. The platypus not only looked like no animal ever seen or imagined before, but its habits and characteristics were every bit as peculiar. It was furry and produced milk like a mammal, but it laid tough-skinned eggs like a reptile and was able to feed only under water, like a duck. One exasperated scientist, confronted by this persistent defiance of the natural world as he knew it, gave up and named the zoologically perverse animal *paradoxus* for its contradictory makeup.

In time the platypus and its only known relatives, the spiny anteaters, or echidnas, were recognized as the lone members of an exclusive order of mammals called monotremes, which in fact represent a kind of midpoint on the ladder of evolution between reptiles and mammals. Like lizards and crocodiles, the platypus and spiny anteaters have legs that splay out to the side rather than supporting their bodies from underneath. The male platypus has a poison spur (on the hind leg) that emits venom. But the brain of a monotreme is larger and more complex than that of a reptile, the heart is more highly developed and the body hair marks monotremes as warm-blooded mammals. Scientists, lacking fossil evidence that would clearly establish monotreme ancestry, can only speculate. Their theory: The platypus and spiny anteaters may be the sole surviving descendants of a species that linked reptiles to mammals on the chain of evolution millions of years ago.

Platypuses live in burrows they dig out of riverbanks in the damper precincts of eastern Australia and Tasmania —and absolutely nowhere else. A few were brought to New York's Bronx Zoo some years ago, but the last ones died in the late 1950s and were not replaced. A male measures about 18 inches long with another six inches of flat, beaverlike tail. The long, curved claws facilitate digging, while the webbing between claws opens out to form efficient paddles in the water. Platypuses search river and lake bottoms for worms, crustaceans and other small aquatic animals, which they locate with their sensitive bills. They feed with such gusto that they have been known to consume their weight in food in a night. One captive platypus required 1,200 worms and 50 crayfish every 24 hours. The young are hatched in a bark-and-leaf-lined nursery several yards deep within a special breeding warren. Only a half inch long at birth, they lap up milk that is secreted like perspiration on the mother's belly and stay with their mother until they are about 17 weeks old and a foot long, when they leave for their first swim.

Duckbills were hunted to near extinction by 19th-century trappers who coveted their dark, molelike fur. They occasionally perished in fish traps as well. As a result the Australian government placed them under rigid protection. In recent years some populations have actually begun to increase.

Unlike platypuses, spiny anteaters can thrive in a variety of habitats. They have penetrated every Australian land environment short of open desert and also live in Tasmania and New Guinea. The secret of their proliferation may be their lack of appeal to human appetites. No one but aborigines has ever been enthusiastic about their meat, which smells of formic acid from their diet of ants and termites. Their sharp-spined, porcupinelike coats hold no charm for furriers.

Female echidnas have managed to preserve a singular mystery about themselves—how they are able to deposit their eggs into a small, rearward-opening pouch that develops temporarily on their underside during incubation. The creatures have surprising strength for their weight (up to 22 pounds). One specimen, locked in a scientist's kitchen overnight, moved every piece of furniture away from the wall except for a stove that was anchored by a pipe. When alarmed, a spiny anteater has the ability to scrabble furiously with all of its formidable claws and sink into the earth with the dispatch of a descending elevator. All that remains at ground level is an inch-high tussock of quill tips, masquerading as grass.

Prickly Primitives

Members of the monotreme family, along with the platypus (pages 84–85), are five species of spiny anteaters, popularly called echidnas. The spiny anteater's roly-poly body is a bristling pincushion of sharp spines that protect the animal so effectively that it boldly forages for food during the daylight hours, seemingly confident that it can withstand any threat.

Ants, termites and worms are the echidna's principal diet, which it laps up rapidly with its long, probing tongue. Covering the tongue are ridges and a sticky substance that holds the insects fast; both help the toothless monotreme to manage its meal.

During the breeding season the female spiny anteater develops a temporary pouch along the midline of her belly in which the single egg is placed immediately after it is laid. The pouch serves as a womb during the seven- to 10-day incubation of the egg and then as a nursing pouch for her growing youngster. The pouch disappears when the young become independent at about 10 weeks.

In this sequence of pictures (opposite, top to bottom) a spiny anteater demonstrates its skill at eluding foes by burying itself quickly in the soft earth so that nothing but a small, spiky and virtually impregnable mound remains visible.

A young spiny anteater (above, right), with the spines of its coat just beginning to sprout, struggles to navigate along a tree limb. When they begin to develop spines, at about six weeks, the young anteaters are placed in a nest and continue to nurse until they are finally left to seek their own nourishment—when their prickles have grown long enough to protect them.

Clutching a branch in its four claw-tipped paws, a spiny anteater (right) prepares to lick it clean of termites. Echidnas crush their food between their tongues and the ridged roofs of their mouths.

Duck-billed Submariner

The freshwater streams and lakes of eastern Australia and Tasmania are the home of the platypus. Looking like a hodgepodge of parts that have been taken from many different animals, the platypus (opposite and above) is a highly specialized creature that is superbly suited for its amphibious way of life.

Its webbed feet provide propulsion through the water, while its paddlelike tail acts as a rudder. Ears and eyes are set in deep clefts in the skin. When the platypus submerges, the edges surrounding these recesses close around the organs, waterproofing them effectively but also rendering the platypus blind and deaf. Then the platypus's sense of touch, embodied in its splendid bill, takes over. Unlike the horny beaks of birds, the platypus's bill is a bony frame covered with soft, moist skin. Naked of fur, it is lined with numerous nerve endings that make it a highly sensitive underwater instrument for guiding the platypus down waterways, around rocks and logs and in and out of thick aquatic vegetation in pursuit of such prey as worms, tadpoles and crustaceans.

Following the Equator

by Mark Twain

In an account of his trip around the world in 1895, Mark Twain presented to his readers a remarkable old Australian naturalist who in turn described the "grotesquest of animals, king of the animalculae of the world for versatility of character and make-up." Here is Mark Twain's platypus.

You can call it anything you want to, and be right. It is a fish, for it lives in the river half the time; it is a land-animal, for it resides on the land half the time; it is an amphibian, since it likes both and does not know which it prefers; it is a hybernian, for when times are dull and nothing much going on it buries itself under the mud at the bottom of a puddle and hybernates there a couple of weeks at a time; it is a kind of duck, for it has a duck-bill and four webbed paddles; it is a fish and quadruped together, for in the water it swims with the paddles and on shore it paws itself across country with them; it is a kind of seal, for it has a seal's fur; it is carnivorous, herbivorous, insectivorous, and vermifuginous, for it eats fish and grass and butterflies, and in the season digs worms out of the mud and devours them; it is clearly a bird, for it lays eggs and hatches them; it is clearly a mammal, for it nurses its young; and it is manifestly a kind of Christian, for it keeps the Sabbath when there is anybody around, and when there isn't, doesn't. It has all the tastes there are except refined ones, it has all the habits there are except good ones.

It is a survival—a survival of the fittest. Mr. Darwin invented the theory that goes by that name, but the Ornithorhyncus was the first to put it to actual experiment and prove that it could be done. Hence it should have as much of the credit as Mr. Darwin. It was never in the Ark; you will find no mention of it there; it nobly stayed out and worked the theory. Of all creatures in the world it was the only one properly equipped for the test. The Ark was thirteen months afloat, and all the globe submerged; no land visible above the flood, no vegetation, no food for a mammal to eat, nor water for a mammal to drink; for all mammal food was destroyed, and when the pure floods from heaven and the salt oceans of the earth mingled their waters and rose above the mountain-tops, the result was a drink which no bird or beast of ordinary construction could use and live. But this combination was nuts for the Ornithorhyncus, if I may use a term like that without offense. Its river home had always been salted by the flood-tides of the sea. On the face of the Noachian deluge innumerable forest trees were floating. Upon these the Ornithorhyncus voyaged in peace; voyaged from clime to clime, from hemisphere to hemisphere, in contentment and comfort, in virile interest in the constant change of scene, in humble thankfulness for its privileges, in ever-increasing enthusiasm in the development of the great theory upon

whose validity it had staked its life, its fortunes, and its sacred honor, if I may use such expressions without impropriety in connection with an episode of this nature.

It lived the tranquil and luxurious life of a creature of independent means. Of things actually necessary to its existence and its happiness not a detail was wanting. When it wished to walk, it scrambled along the tree-trunk; it mused in the shade of the leaves by day, it slept in their shelter by night; when it wanted the refreshment of a swim, it had it; it ate leaves when it wanted a vegetable diet, it dug under the bark for worms and grubs; when it wanted fish it caught them, when it wanted eggs it laid them. If the grubs gave out in one tree it swam to another; and as for fish, the very opulence of the supply was an embarrassment. And finally, when it was thirsty it smacked its chops in gratitude over a blend that would have slain a crocodile.

When at last, after thirteen months of travel and research in all the Zones, it went aground on a mountain-summit, it strode ashore, saying in its heart, "Let them that come after me invent theories and dream dreams about the Survival of the Fittest if they like, but I am the first that has *done* it!"

This wonderful creature dates back, like the kangaroo and many other Australian hydrocephalous invertebrates, to an age long anterior to the advent of man upon the earth; they date back, indeed, to a time when a causeway, hundreds of miles wide and thousands of miles long, joined Australia to Africa, and the animals of the two countries were alike, and all belonged to that remote geological epoch known to science as the Old Red Grindstone Post-Pleosaurian. Later the causeway sank under the sea; subterranean convulsions lifted the African continent a thousand feet higher than it was before, but Australia kept her old level. In Africa's new climate the animals necessarily began to develop and shade off into new forms and families and species, but the animals of Australia as necessarily remained stationary, and have so remained until this day. In the course of some millions of years the African Ornithorhyncus developed and developed and developed, and sloughed off detail after detail of its make-up until at last the creature became wholly disintegrated and scattered. Whenever you see a bird or a beast or a seal or an otter in Africa you know that he is merely a sorry surviving fragment of that sublime original of whom I have been speaking—that creature which was everything in general and nothing in particular—the opulently endowed *e pluribus unum* of the animal world.

Such is the history of the most hoary, the most ancient, the most venerable creature that exists in the earth to-day —*Ornithorhyncus Platypus Extraordinariensis*—whom God preserve!

Reptiles

A traveler in the Australian bush may take some comfort in the knowledge that there are no large, dangerous mammals to worry about—no grizzly bears, no gorillas, no lions or tigers or leopards. The biggest native beast is the gentle kangaroo. But the seasoned bush explorer always checks the rocks and hollow logs around his campsite. Snakes are the danger Down Under.

Australian snakes are no fiercer or more combative than their counterparts on other continents—the Indian cobra, for example, or the rattlesnake of North America. But it is a curious fact that about 65 of 110 species of snakes in Australia are venomous, a higher proportion than anyplace else. The island continent has in fact the dubious distinction of being the only place on earth where venomous snakes outnumber the harmless varieties. It must be added that most of these pack a relatively weak poison and are no threat to humans, but a half dozen or so are dangerous indeed, and among them are some of the most formidable reptiles ever evolved. There are in addition some 30 species of venomous sea snakes in Australian coastal waters, likely to be encountered only by fishermen using nets.

The most lethal snake of Australia is the taipan, which is dark-brown-backed, yellow-bellied and averages about eight feet in length. The taipan's range is in northern Australia, the most tropical part of the country, and in New Guinea. Taipans have a high tolerance for heat, more so than many other snakes, and are active in the heat of day as well as at night. Their deadly potency—as great for their size as for any other reptile on earth—is illustrated by an awesome statistic: The venom reserves of an average taipan are sufficient to kill 200 sheep or 23,000 mice. The American copperhead, by comparison, has enough venom to slay eight sheep, and the Indian cobra is a potential killer of 31. A taipan's normal prey includes rats, small bandicoots, birds and mice. It shows no inclination to attack people unless it is molested, despite folk tales about its aggressiveness.

Legends about taipans and other lethal Australian snakes flourish: They can strip the milk from cows; a snake will avenge the death of its mate; music will entice them from their lairs; they swallow their young to protect them. The taipan, however, needs no myths to inflate its reputation. Lacking antivenom serum, and sometimes even if serum is available, the victim of its bite usually dies.

Several Australian snakes, including taipans, engage in spectacular wrestling matches during the mating season. Male snakes chase one another across the ground, twining around one another and crawling frantically through the bushes, stopping to lift their bodies high and writhing in a bizarre dance. The prize is territorial dominance. The Australian brown snake is a particularly vigorous wrestler, coiling so tightly around its adversary that the battlers look like a twin-strand rope. After the fight the loser slinks off, but the bouts are sometimes repeated daily for as long as a month.

Tiger snakes, smaller than taipans and almost as lethal, have been responsible for more human deaths because they are more likely to occur in populated areas. Their feed is chiefly frogs and mice. Up to 109 young are born live at a time, each measuring about nine inches long. At birth a tiger snake, like most other snakes, is on its own, and it immediately assumes a striking stance.

The death adder is a deadly attacker from close range when disturbed. It uses its tail as a lure, twitching it to attract lizards and birds into striking range. Death adders are looked on as a special menace by Australian sheepherders, for they will kill any sheep that tramples on them.

Of the nonvenomous Australian snakes the most impressive are the pythons, particularly the amethystine python, which can grow as long as 28 feet and squeeze the life out of a 50-pound kangaroo. Nocturnal pythons and death adders have better night vision than the other snakes. The most significant enemies of Australian snakes are large birds of prey such as eagles and hawks, and brush fires, which seem to paralyze snakes and leave them helpless.

Snakes may be the lurking menaces of the bush, but dragon lizards certainly look more villainous. Relatively harmless except to smaller lizards, frogs and insects, these often large reptiles look like survivors of the dinosaur age. The frilled-neck dragon, when excited, opens a parasol of skin that may be a foot across, ranging in hue from bright pink through orange to black. Another dragon, known as the thorny devil or moloch, has hard cone-shaped bristles all over its body.

Australia has a variety of legless lizards, indistinguishable from snakes at a casual glance. Most have external ear openings, but others, more snakelike than the rest, lack distinguishing characteristics. All, however, show to at least a slight degree a pair of small flaps of skin that are the vestiges of their ancestral hind limbs.

Goanna lizard

Diurnal Dragons

Primitive and dragonlike in appearance, monitor lizards, commonly called goannas in Australia, are a hardy family of lizards that can live in almost any environment, dry or wet, providing sufficient warmth. Goannas are distinguished by tapered heads, long slender necks and four powerful legs, each ending in five clawed toes. Their tails, often twice as long as their bodies, propel the animals when they swim and are effective as defensive weapons. All monitors are diurnal and reach their peak of activity when the sun is high, pursuing and feeding on a wide range of other animals: Monitors prey on lizards, frogs, birds, rats, snakes, fish, insects and crustaceans. After eating, a monitor performs a ritual. It licks its snout with its tongue, rubs the sides of its head against the ground and finally raises its head and surveys the terrain for fresh prey—or danger.

Of the world's total of 31 monitor species, Australia has about 20, and 17 are found only in that continent. The most prevalent species is *Varanus gouldii*, commonly known as Gould's goanna, which inhabits almost all of Australia. The largest is the perentie, *Varanus giganteus*, which reaches a length of eight feet.

Varanus gouldii, or Gould's goanna (right), is the speediest of the Australian monitors and has earned the title of "the racehorse goanna." In the rugged Down Under terrain it can easily outdistance a man over a short stretch. When on the defensive it raises itself on a tripod formed by its hind legs and tail.

Semiaquatic, Varanus mertensi (below) retreats to water when it senses danger. An excellent swimmer, it steers in the water with its laterally flattened tail.

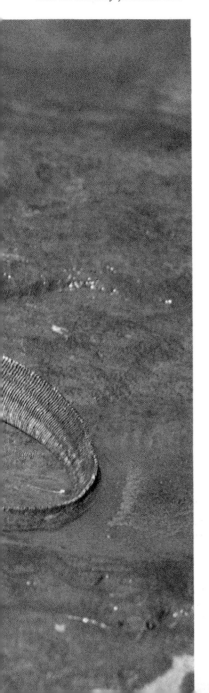

Murray Walkabout

by Archer Russell

In the Australian vernacular, the expression "walkabout" means more than a stroll. The word signifies a kind of retreat from the pressures of urban life and a return to the simpler, quieter ways of the bush country. The idea appealed strongly to the Australian nature writer Archer Russell, who embarked on a walkabout with a group of friends along the Murray River in southeastern Australia. Russell's record of the journey, entitled Murray Walkabout, *includes tales about the local people that he and his party met and the animal life that often shared their campsites. Their favorite guest was a large goanna—a shaggy-looking lizard that they promptly named "Old Ragged Coat."*

Awakened one dark night by what sounded like the tearing of paper, I slipped quietly from my sleeping-bag, grasped my rabbit-gun, and crept stealthily but belligerently towards the larder. It had occurred to me that a fox or wild cat might be nosing among the provender. But there was nothing there.

At the first peep of day, however, the outrage stood revealed in all its shabby banditry. Ten feet from the larder, its wrappings completely torn away, lay our precious butter-jar as empty of its contents as an egg after breakfast; while leading to and fro from the larder were the tell-tale tracks of a huge sand monitor, or goanna.

This goanna, from his natural haunts among the scrubs and cliffs, found our camp particularly inviting during that season. He was a giant of a reptile, with a body as thick round the middle as the biceps of Samson's arm, and nearly six feet long. For a time he was the most disreputable-looking fellow you ever did see. Undergoing the annual process of shedding his old coat for a new one, he was more ragged and tattery than a year-old scarecrow. But for all his moulting, he was agile enough, striding about the camp like some ancient dinosaur, or clawing his way up the boles and branches above our cooking place as though he were some demon of the trees—as indeed, in a way, he was.

Between the goanna and the soldier-birds about our camp there was perpetual war. From that hard old dominie Experience, the birds knew exactly what "Old Ragged Coat," as Miranda christened him, was about, or would ultimately be about. If he escaped our eyes the soldier-birds soon told us where he lurked. There is no bird in the scrubs more capable of warning the wild of a back-stairs danger. In alertness and aggressiveness against potential foes—snakes, lizards, and owls—and in the habit it has of waging united war upon any real or supposed intruder of its domains, the soldier-bird is a regular firebrand. Of course we all know what a predatory old rascal the goanna is: how in the depths of his banditry he seeks to prey upon the eggs and young of brooding birds, both in the trees and on the ground; and it is this, no doubt, that brings upon his scaly head so much assault and battery. A wild outburst of squeaking and the soldier-bird flock is beside itself; it

has spied "Old Ragged Coat" as he makes his way up a cliff-side gum tree. Invasion demands action; this is war. With beating wings and clamorous cries the birds dart upon the intruder; not a soldier-bird within hearing but hastens to the scene, to join in the mêlée as if obeying some primordial instinct of defence. So the attack goes on, until, wearied and baffled, the goanna turns about and claws his way warily to the ground. These stinging attacks cost "Old Ragged Coat" many an anxious and irritating hour.

There were few items in our programme of events of which this lovable old reprobate was not cognizant. I have strong suspicions that his liking for our camping ground was the equal of our own. No doubt he watched us from the trees. Be that as it may, seldom did we move out but "Old Ragged Coat" moved in. We rather liked to think he did, and would have condoned it at all times but for his irrepressible industry. Arrived within the camp, he would begin mining operations on a large scale somewhat on the "open cut" system. That would not have mattered much had he confined his industry to the floor of the sandbank. But he did no such thing; he devoted it entirely to the floor of the tent: for "Old Ragged Coat's" *tour de force* was not so stupid as it looked. He dug those two-feet-deep holes to lie in, and he dug them inside the tent because the sand beneath it was cooler than the sand outside, which was heated by the direct rays of the sun. Yet he was harmless enough; all Australian lizards are, unless molested. Not one is in any way venomous, although a bite from the goanna, owing to the coating of putrefactive matter on the jaws, will sometimes set up a septic condition. . . .

But let us return to "Old Ragged Coat," of which we both, Miranda in particular, retain the liveliest memories. As Miranda and I stood on the riverside one sizzling day, watching a steamboat pass, we noticed on the surface of the

water, floating down on the slow current, a stick-like object which we at first mistook for a small dry branch that had fallen into the river from some overhanging tree. We had seen many such floating sticks before and had given little heed to them; but somehow this particular stick seemed different from the ordinary run of sticks. We were right; it was. Suddenly the "stick" became vigorously and unmistakably alive; the creature, whatever it was, had caught the sound of the steamer's paddles. However, once out of the steamer's course, it threw no more than a furtive glance at the passing boat, and went drifting down the stream again. It was "Old Ragged Coat" enjoying a summer "cool off."

Miranda did not like her old friend pushing off into the stream again. It savoured too much of misadventure. The creature was drowning; even now it was in its death throes; and nothing that I could say or do would convince Miranda to the contrary. "Quick!" she cried, "we must put out in the flattie and save it."

Never shall I forget the look "Old Ragged Coat" shot at us as we pushed towards him. "A pest on these humans," he seemed to say. "But wait, perhaps they haven't seen me. I'll camouflage, anyhow."

And camouflage he did; inverting his long tail, he lay motionless on the surface of the water, a lifeless stick again, but with eyes that watched every turn and movement we made. And so he remained until, at Miranda's frantic urging, I sought to lift him into the boat.

A flurry of foam and he was gone; a flash and he had scuttled up the bank, lost in a maze of protruding gum roots. It was as quick as that. I don't quite know to this day what Miranda said. Anyhow, a man with a grain of sense wouldn't repeat it even if he did. But can you imagine a situation more inherently comic?

Geckos and Skinks

Geckos and skinks, two families of lizards, are found in tropical and subtropical regions around the earth. All Australian geckos and some skinks have tails that they can shed at will as a defense mechanism. They can also draw on their tails as reservoirs of fat that tide them over periods when the insects they eat are scarce. Of more than 60 species of geckos on the continent, most are less than four inches in length and are almost exclusively nocturnal. They have large, round, lidless eyes protected by transparent spectacles, which they clean by licking with their long tongues. Geckos are the only lizards that regularly vocal-ize, and they are highly regarded as insect and scorpion controls. The leaf-tailed gecko (opposite, left) is a master of camouflage; its skin is the color of bark, and its flanks and limbs have a border of scales. Pressed flat against a tree, it is virtually invisible.

Skinks abound in Australia, where there are close to 200 species. Typical skinks are slender, smooth, short-limbed, long-tailed ground dwellers. But among Australian skinks there are some species with no legs at all and others, such as the shingleback (opposite right, above), that are large, short-tailed and rough-scaled.

Spiny-tailed gecko

Northern leaf-tailed gecko

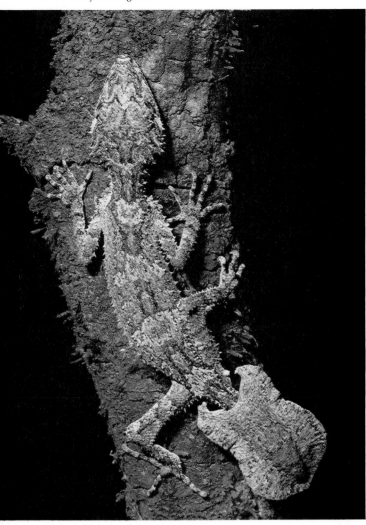

Shingleback lizard

Western blue-tongued skink

Knob-tailed gecko

Ferocious-looking but harmless, a frilled lizard
(below), native to Australia and New Guinea,
demonstrates its threat display. The raised collar
around its neck is a fold of scaly skin supported by
cartilage; except for threat or courtship display, it is
kept flattened against the body. When the frill is
expanded the lizard usually enhances the effect by
rising on its two hind legs, hissing with mouth wide
open and whipping its tail back and forth menacingly.
A mature, three-foot-long male may have a frill that
measures 10 inches across.

Two Australian lizards known as molochs or thorny
devils search for black ants, virtually the sole item in
their diet. In spite of its forbidding appearance, the
thorny devil is a lethargic, harmless creature,
remarkably adapted to desert life. The nodule behind its
head probably serves as a fat reserve that can be
metabolized to provide water during dry periods. In
addition, the scales of the thorny devil are separated by
tiny threadlike canals that instantly absorb any
available water. The canals reach the corners of the
moloch's mouth, where it imbibes the water by moving its
jaws. An inhabitant of Australian deserts and plains, the
moloch is a prime example of convergence. Although it
strongly resembles the horned lizards of the American
Southwest—also creatures of hot, arid environments
—the two are completely unrelated.

98

Shy but Deadly

An unexpected brush with either of the venom-laden snakes shown on these pages is one of the most dangerous encounters a traveler in Australia can experience. The taipan and tiger snakes are members of the Elapidae, or cobra family, to which about 60 percent of all the snakes in Australia belong. The largest of Australia's venomous snakes, the taipan (opposite) is reputedly the world's most poisonous. It grows to a length of 13 feet and is coppery brown to chocolate brown on its upper surfaces and cream speckled with orange on the underside. The taipan is normally timid and retiring, but when provoked it becomes ferocious. Agile, it can strike from a considerable distance and often plunges its fangs into several places in rapid succession. Its venom is one of the most potent toxins known. Before the development of modern snakebite remedies, called antivenenes, about 80 percent of taipan bites were fatal. Death occurs from paralysis of the nerve centers controlling the lungs and heart.

Drop for drop, the venom of a tiger snake (below) is even more toxic, but its fangs are relatively short, and the quantity injected from a single bite is small. Found primarily in swampy areas in the south of Australia, the tiger snake varies greatly in color and may be brown, black or yellowish with dark transverse bands. Its body is relatively heavy and it has a substantial head. Like the taipan, it is usually shy, but when aroused it attacks vigorously.

The Squeezers

Australia and the adjacent islands not only have the largest proportion of venomous snakes in the world, but the region also harbors a large concentration of constrictors—10 species of Old World pythons, including the two impressive specimens shown here. The carpet python—*Python spilotus* (pages 104–107)—is a single species that appears with two very differently marked color phases: yellow-splotched (right) and gray and blue-black with diamond patterns. Where their habitats merge, the two subspecies often interbreed, resulting in an even more bewildering array of markings. Carpet snakes are voracious predators on small animals and birds and are sometimes confined in Australian barns and silos as effective rat catchers.

Although carpet snakes reach a maximum size of 10 to 14 feet, the amethystine python (below) has been measured at a documented length of 28 feet and ranks with the closely related reticulated python of Southeast Asia and the anaconda of South America as one of the true giants among snakes. Although the relatively slender amethystines sometimes eat wallabies and kangaroos and are quite capable of squeezing a man to death, they are elusive creatures, not regarded as a menace to humans.

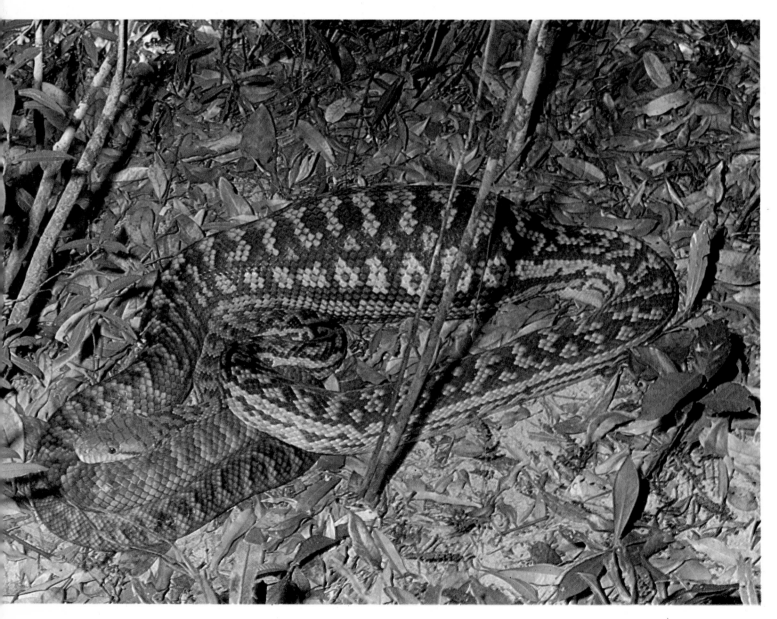

My Crowded Solitude

by Jack McLaren

Off Cape York, the northernmost point of the Australian mainland, a small spit of land juts out amid the islands of the Torres Strait. It was here in 1911 that Australian pioneer Jack McLaren and an equally adventurous and enterprising friend decided to try to start the area's first coconut plantation. McLaren built himself a spacious house with a cane-covered veranda that extended along the front and sides. Here he lived in peaceful seclusion with his bull terrier, Togo, until one terrifying night he awakened to find his isolation invaded by a tremendous carpet snake. McLaren's and Togo's battle with this deadly intruder is recounted in this excerpt from his book My Crowded Solitude.

I had only a glimpse of the other room, for the gasometer was empty, and there was only a breath of gas in the pipes, but the flicker of light was sufficient to show me, in the middle of the floor, making straight for the sleeping dog, a carpet snake a full two fathoms long. I shouted, and Togo awoke at once into barking and snapping and snarling activity and much rushing hither and thither; then the gas gave its final flicker and went out, but not before I saw the snake make for the wall and up towards the roof. Evidently it considered that while a dog asleep was one thing, a dog very much awake and filled with active antagonism was another thing altogether.

I made a bonfire of matches on the table which occupied the centre of the room. To have recharged the gasometer would have taken such a time that the snake would probably have disappeared before I finished. The bonfire of matches discovered for me the snake lying along the ridge-pole of the house; and when with a spear that hung on the wall I had poked it till its head was in such position as to allow me to get at it, I shot it—both barrels of a 12-bore shot-gun. And with that the snake's great long length came down and down, till it hung straight over the table and the flaring of the matches like a mighty rope. And then it stopped. Despite that its head was shot almost completely away, it was still filled with life and vigour, and with the end of its tail had taken a good, strong grip of the ridge-pole.

Togo sprang up on the table and sunk his teeth in it. I beat at it with the gun. I jabbed the spear into it. I was more than a little unstrung. Those long weeks of solitude had affected my nerves. That horrible, slightly-swaying rope was something from a place of slimy demons. In the now flickering light its diamond patterns shone like dreadful eyes; when a match exploded they gave quick and vicious gleamings. I could have screamed. I think I did scream. Blood from its shot head dripped on to the bonfire, spluttering. Snake's blood! Frenzied, I beat at its thick, long length; then I dropped both gun and spear and grasped it with my hands and pulled.

Then suddenly the thing released its grip of the ridge and came tumbling down in a mighty monstrous mass that blotted out the bonfire and splashed my face with blood; and the next moment I was hanging on to the doorpost as never I had hung on to anything before, for in falling the Thing had taken around my arm a full round turn, covering it from elbow to shoulder, and with its tail got a grip the further side of the table in order to give it "purchase" —and was constricting with all its strength. I know I screamed now. I remember screaming, distinctly. The great coil about my arm was hard as iron, and as cold. It was a little slimy. I felt the muscles tauten against mine. The power was terrific. My arm was paralysed. My reason was paralysed. I tried to bite that awful coil. It was like

biting steel. With my bare foot I tried to wrench my arm sidewise and free. I knew these efforts were futile. Still, I tried them. And all the while that cold, hard grip became harder, and seemingly colder. The pain must have been very great; but I was not aware of it. Mental shock had rendered physical shock subservient.

The Thing's half head hung down from my arm a little way. The blood from it dripped on my foot. My sarong came off, fell on my foot and caught the blood instead. I was thankful for that. Togo was snapping at the head, now and then gripping it and pulling. Sometimes he brushed my naked leg; and the warmth of his body felt gratifying after the coldness of the coil about my arm. I shouted words of encouragement and praise to him, though why I should have shouted them I did not know, for, willing though he was, he could do nothing.

Then, when it seemed to me I had clung to the doorpost for hours—though it was really only a few moments, as I saw afterwards by my watch—and when my arm was near the breaking, the coil began to slacken. With the pull of the snake upon it, the table was turning over. The snake was losing its "purchase." A moment later the table crashed over, the coil slackened completely, dropped heavily to the floor, and my arm was free. I sprang into my bedroom, found some matches and struck one. The Thing was making slowly out of the main doorway, on to the veranda, Togo still hanging at its head. By the time it had reached the ground, where I could see it more or less plainly in the clear darkness, I was ready and waiting for it, and with a dozen charges of buckshot blew it to pieces. Then I recharged the gasometer, and lay in the brightness of the light till daylight, trembling as from fever or from cold, afraid to shut my eyes for fear I should see again that monstrous, gleaming rope. And for many nights afterwards I lay fitfully awake because of thoughts of it, while as for Togo, I am sure he knew full well that he himself had been the object of the snake's intrusion of the house, for often he would awaken with a short and sudden yelp and spring up bristling, exactly as though he, too, had imagined a quiet rustling on the Papuan mats of the floor.

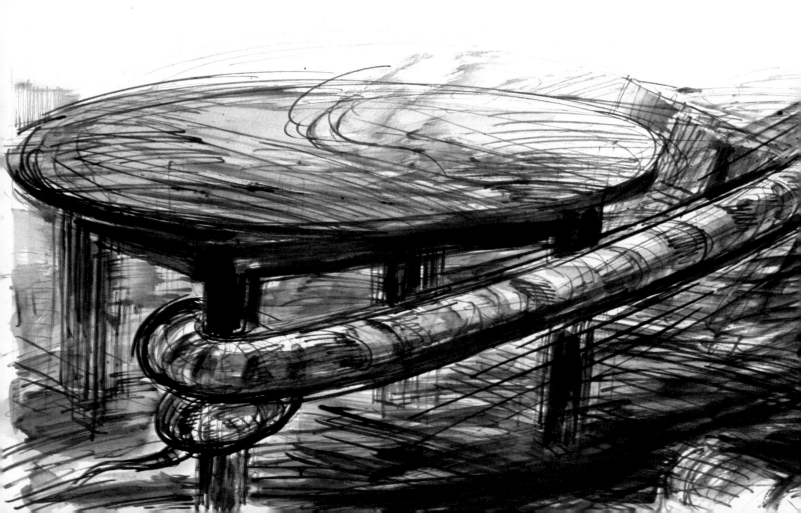

Birds

Bowerbirds, which build little tepees of dirt, paint the walls with berry juice and cultivate their own moss gardens; busy mallee fowls, scrambling for most of the year to make and maintain a temperature-controlled incubation chamber; gaudy, show-business lyrebirds, all song and mimicry and dazzle; flightless cassowaries with their jagged, bony helmets, green eyebrows and purple necks; emus, the grounded six-footers of the desert and bush—the bird life of Australia and its neighboring islands is breathtaking, among the most colorful and impressive anywhere. The Australian mainland has 750 species of birds—a number that compares favorably with the total in all of North America. Indeed, an early map identified Australia as *terra psittacorum*—land of parrots—in recognition of the budgerigars, lories and cockatoos that are found only in the island continent and its dependencies.

Male bowerbirds build their tunnels and central chambers out of ground cover and twigs and then decorate them with whatever bright material suits their fancy—feathers, shells, fruits, pieces of glass, campground litter. The purpose is to entice the female inside, or at least to the front yard. If the love nest he has made doesn't satisfy her, a bowerbird, depending on species, might add pebble-lined walkways or a moss garden. Sometimes he makes a sort of paint from charcoal or berries and applies it to the bower's walls with a wad of leaves or bark. Then he waits anxiously while the female looks it over and either enters the bower or moves on. And even after all that effort the female invariably leaves after mating and builds her own nest.

Lyrebirds take a different route to the same goal. During the mating season the male constructs a series of platforms of soil raked up from the forest floor, placing them in as many as 10 or more clearings as showcases for his courtship performances. He struts around, opening up his silvery, lyre-shaped tail, and sings his heart out. The repertoire includes not only his own song but also pitch-perfect imitations of other birds and of every sound he has ever heard, sometimes including factory whistles, auto horns or machinery. He dances as he sings, swaying from side to side. After courtship and mating, however, the male leaves the chores of incubating and rearing the young to the female.

Lyrebirds have well-developed voices even as chicks. If a chick is disturbed in its twig-roofed nest, it will react by pressing itself out of sight against the roof. If this fails to dissuade an intruder, it cuts loose with a high-pitched shriek so loud that it rattles nearby branches and brings its mother winging to the rescue.

Some ornithologists believe that lyrebirds are closely related to the brightly spangled birds of paradise of New Guinea, with whom they share their splendid plumage and instinct for display. Some of the 43 bird of paradise species were named after European royalty by early Down Under colonists who hoped for favors in return—from the Kaiserine of Germany, for example. As in the case of lyrebirds, the male birds of paradise sing and dance for the females, and the best performer may mate with a dozen females in a season.

The most extraordinary of the remarkable Down Under birds, however, may be the mallee fowl of the sagelike scrub country of southern Australia. The mallee may be the wild world's most hard-working father. His work begins in April or May, the Southern Hemisphere's autumn, when he and his mate excavate a hole into which they pack leaves and twigs. When winter rain has dampened this heat-productive compost, the mallees pile two or three feet of sand atop it to seal in the moisture and warmth. Deep within the mound is a special chamber for the eggs.

In September the female then begins a cycle of egg-laying that produces an average of an egg a week for as long as six months. During this time it is the male's constant task to regulate the temperature of the incubation chamber. His thermometer is apparently the sensitive inner part of his bill and his tongue, which he periodically pokes into the mound. If the fermenting vegetation and air temperature cause the chamber temperature to rise above 96° F., he digs away the sandy covering and lets the complex cool in the evening. If it goes below 90° he either piles on more sand at night or digs it away during the day, exposing it to the warmth of the sun. Sometimes he must alternate. His work is constant, and the male mallee sometimes becomes so overheated that he literally pants.

Finally, with the arrival of autumn the chamber temperature drops too low for him to control. His mate stops laying eggs, and he can rest for about a month, when the whole cycle begins again. The strangest part of the mallees' prodigious earth-moving maneuvers is their lack of interest in the result of their labor. Neither parent shows any concern for the hatched offspring. Once out of their eggs, the chicks claw their way out of their underground cradles. When they reach the surface they are on their own.

Count Raggi's bird of paradise

Found in the coastal mountain forests of eastern Australia, the superb lyrebird (left) is famed for its long silvery tail and its amazing mimicry of other birds' calls. When courting, the male struts in a forest clearing, unfurls its shimmering tail and sings a serenade to attract a mate.

The largest and most remarkable of the forest kingfishers is the kookaburra, shown below holding a lizard in its beak. It will carry the reptile to a perch and then batter it senseless with its massive bill before swallowing it whole.

Only in Australia

Although many of Australia's splendid birds are migratory, commuting from as far away as Siberia and Alaska, there are three stay-at-homes that can be found nowhere else in the world—the emu, the kookaburra and the lyrebird. The long-necked mother and chick at left are emus, the second largest birds in the world—after ostriches—and the only surviving members of the family Dromaius. Three other species of emus that once inhabited Tasmania and two smaller islands are extinct.

Emus grow to a height of five to six feet and weigh as much as 120 pounds. They are flightless but fleet-footed and are capable of running at speeds of 40 miles an hour. Although they eat caterpillars, grasshoppers and the burrs that mat sheep wool—and are thus beneficial to mankind—emus also feed on green grass and herbs, which in Australia are reserved for sheep. During the 1930s, when a 50-cent bounty was offered for every bird, emus were killed in great numbers. In 1937, 37,000 emus were killed in the Northampton district alone. Unlike the emu, the kookaburra (right) is highly regarded because it kills poisonous snakes. One species has been dubbed the laughing jackass for its raucous, strangely human cackle.

The lyrebird (above) was first classified as a gallinaceous bird because its shape so closely resembled that of the pheasant. But its melodious voice and uncanny gift for imitating other bird calls later led to its classification in the passerine order of perching birds.

Bird Wonders of Australia

by Alexander Hugh Chisholm

Many wild creatures appear to their human counterparts as natural entertainers, ready to perform at the least provocation. Such an instinctive ham is the male lyrebird. In 1933 a recording crew of the Australian Broadcasting Commission was fortunate in finding an especially flamboyant performer in a male lyrebird that strolled up to a hidden microphone and unloosed his entire repertoire of singing, mimicking, dancing and tail displaying. Alexander Chisholm, a noted Australian naturalist, was present at the impromptu performance and wrote the following review.

Sitting among shrubs and moss-grown logs in the dimly-lit forest, we heard, during the first half-hour, several glorious bursts of melody from unseen birds. The first impulse then was to say, "How like the gramophone record!" just as someone who heard the British Cuckoo for the first time said, "How like the clock!"

But, it may be asked, why should the voices of these Lyre-birds suggest the gramophone record any more than would the voices of Lyre-birds in other parts of Australia?

That question expresses the surprise that I felt on first hearing the record in question, for the song differed considerably from the melody of all other Lyre-birds I had heard. The basic qualities were akin, and there were just as many borrowings from the songs and calls of other birds; but the recorded bird-voice was less faithful in some of its imitations, and was more given to adaptations, than were the voices of Lyre-birds in New South Wales and Queensland. Certain notes of the Grey Thrush, for example, were glorified far beyond the Thrush standard, and the laughter of the Kookaburra ran off into a wonderful ripple suggesting the sound of water bubbling and babbling over rocks.

All of the Sherbrooke Lyre-birds appear to use these distinctive notes. Were they developed by some master among the mockers of this tight little kingdom, and passed on from one generation to another? If so, why is it that Lyre-birds in other parts are resolute and faithful mimics, but are less inclined to adapt and improvise?

I do not wish to imply, however, that the Sherbrooke Lyre-birds depart from the originals in *all* their vocal borrowings. Much of their mimicry, indeed, is wonderfully exact. In that first half-hour we heard fantasias that contained brilliant imitations of almost every bird-voice of the neighbourhood.

How remarkable it was that these powerful voices could pass from the resounding crack of the Whip-bird to the soft chant of the Pilot-bird; from the wails of the Black and Gang-gang Cockatoos to the melody of the Grey Thrush and the churring of the Yellow Robin; from the laughing notes of the Butcher-bird to the tinkling chatter of a flock of Crimson Parrots! All the voices of the forest were caught into one throat. Listening keenly, we heard even the fragile chatter of the Scrub-Wren and Brown Tit—the voices of birds smaller than Sparrows faithfully imitated by a bird having a body as large as a domestic fowl!

Soon afterwards a warning "Hist!" ran round the small company gathered about the main broadcasting apparatus. Sitting tensely silent, we saw a fine male Lyre-bird stroll on to a mound twenty yards away, and fairly in front of a microphone. For a few seconds he stood in his small arena—a clearing perhaps three feet in diameter, with the soft soil gently elevated—and gazed at us appraisingly. Then the valour of song overcame discretion, and straightway fairy revels began.

What an exquisite performance that was! For the first half-minute or so the master stood at ease as he sang. The voices of a dozen birds of the forest fell easily from a plain brown bird with partly open beak. Pausing for a few moments, he began again; and this time we saw a bird transfigured.

Slowly, majestically, as though responding to the pressure of a secret spring, the great tail began to rise and spread. The two large outer feathers fell away to each side, displaying a beautiful silver-white background and chestnut bars on the under-surface, together with a dainty

black curl at the tip of each. Two long central feathers, grey, slim, gracefully curved, rose and were held at an angle above the back. A mass of fern-like plumes, appearing in an upright position from between the two large outer feathers, created a silvery fan for a moment, and then descended, like an elfin parasol, over the back and the head.

What an astonishing transformation was this! A plain brown bird, through the simple act of spreading and raising the tail so as to display the under-surface, had become beautiful beyond words.

Standing thus, and betimes causing the delicate feathers above the back to quiver and shake in a fairy shower, while the large feathers remained perfectly still, the artist poured out a stream of glorious melody, mingling his natural shouts and gurgles with a copious fantasia of stolen notes. There was no regular sequence in the various series. The talented creature merely took whichever voices occurred to his consciousness, in whatever order, and flung them forth in perfect harmony. But always he favoured that glorified Thrush call and the rippling melody born of the "laughter" of the Kookaburra.

Now came a variation in the fantasy. Swinging into a whimsical chuckle, while still the back and head were obscured by the gauzy filamentary feathers, the master began to "take up his dressing"—to shuffle from side to side. Pausing briefly again, he began a series of rhythmic notes, followed by a quaint little jumping dance.

"Ca-luck, ca-luck!" said the revelling bird.

Immediately on uttering these notes he gave two quaint jumps.

"Ca-luck, ca-luck!" he said again, and again the two jumps followed in perfect time.

"Oooooh!" whispered a small girl who was one of the fascinated audience, "he's skipping pepper."

So the bird proceeded, singing and chortling and dancing, and manifestly enjoying the performance as much as were the spellbound onlookers. As for the rest of Australia—alas! church services were in progress then, and a mere bird-melodist could not be allowed to break in upon the voice of a preacher! But this particular bird was thoroughly obliging; he repeated the performance an hour later and thus people all over Australia were enabled to hear the glorious medley of mockery.

The red-browed pardalote, or diamond bird, shown at left in its burrow nest differs from the majority of flowerpeckers, which feed by probing the hearts of blossoms in search of nectar. Pardalotes live primarily on insects and insect larvae. Moreover, unlike most other flowerpeckers, they do not build elaborate nests in tree branches. Pardalotes either build nests in the hollows of trees or in burrows in the ground.

The female bird feeding its young at left, below, is a flowerpecker that belies the family name with its marked preference for the sticky berries of tropical mistletoes, a taste that has given it the common name of Australian mistletoe bird. The olive-backed sunbird in its snug nest above is an adept architect. Sunbirds build hanging purselike nests woven of plant fibers, bound with spider webs and carefully lined with fur, feathers and down. Both male and female birds take part in building the nest and in the feeding of the young, which usually hatch from a pair of finely speckled white eggs.

A Taste of Honey

An appetite for the nectar of flowering trees and insects is the common denominator of the three families of small to medium-sized perchers and songbirds shown on these pages—honey eaters, sunbirds and flowerpeckers. Found throughout the southwestern Pacific but particularly abundant in Australia, honey eaters often have down-curved bills and long extensible tongues with brushlike tips. The sides of the tongue turn inward to form a tube through which they suck nectar from flowers.

The helmeted friarbird above, one of the largest of the honey eaters, has a vulturelike head, a black bill and red eyes. The sides of its face are bare of feathers, and its body plumage is gray-brown. Shown at top right, feasting on the flower of a banksia tree, the red wattlebird, unlike most honey eaters, also has a taste for fruit as well as nectar and insects. At one time wattlebirds were a favorite target for hunters, who savored their delicious flesh, but they are now protected throughout most of Australia. The New Holland honey eater and the white-plumed honey eater at right are active, noisy birds that make an outlandish racket when they gather together in the eucalyptuses.

Architects of the Bush

Two groups of Australian birds—bowerbirds and mega-podes, or mound-builders, which include the mallee fowl—are outstanding members of the guild of animals, headed by man, that engage in construction. Of the 19 species of bowerbirds all but the three catbirds qualify as accomplished architects.

The male builds a nuptial bower from bits of twigs, grass stalks and other plant materials and decorates them with shells, seeds, berries, flowers, bleached bones and mosses. His work completed, the male displays himself in front of the bower to entice the female inside, or just out front,

where they mate. The female plays no part in the building, and the bower is never used as a nest.

The megapodes, or mound builders, are the only warm-blooded animals that do not rely on their own body heat to incubate their eggs. Most inhabit tropical rain forests, where abundant leaf debris and the humid climate allow the male birds to superintend the incubation of their young in huge thermal mounds of decaying vegetation. The hardy mallee fowl of southern Australia, however, must work much harder to incubate its young in a semidesert area of low rainfall and wide extremes of temperature.

The satin bowerbird at right is the most accomplished of the avenue builders. Having constructed a bower, the male bird paints the interior. He takes a piece of bark in his beak and uses it as a brush to apply a pigment made from fruit juice, charcoal and saliva to the walls of the bower. With an instinctive sense of color dynamics, he creates a unique mating chamber for the female he hopes to attract.

A female mallee fowl oversees her mate at work in their excavated nest (left). The male digs a pit during the rainy autumn, fills it with wet leaves, twigs and grass in early winter and then covers it with sand. When the rotting vegetation has generated enough heat in the late winter, he scoops out a hole, where the mallee hen lays her first egg. The male constantly removes or replaces sand to regulate the temperature until the chicks are hatched.

A great bowerbird (left) bends over to pick up a shell that he has collected for his bower. Some bowerbirds are called avenue builders because the males construct two parallel walls of shell-adorned sticks as one of the settings for their courtship displays. With the last decorative shell in place, the great bowerbird will strut outside his creation and twist his neck to attract the female to the bridal suite.

117

The Durable Budgies

The colorful birds arrayed like little green apples on the branches of the tree above are budgerigars. Highly gregarious, they are the world's most popular cage birds and pets of families from Maine to Madagascar. So many millions of households keep the native Australian birds that it is difficult to believe that the first living budgerigars were brought to England from Down Under only 137 years ago. Since that time they have been bred around the world by the millions. Yellow, blue, white, gray, violet and piebald mutants have been developed from the native green birds.

In their homeland budgerigars breed from October to December. The young are born pink, blind and naked. After eight days the eyes open, a development followed a short time later by the appearance of the first feathers, and before the fifth week the young birds leave the nest. They are fed by their parents for a few additional days, then fly off. In their arid Australian habitat life is a struggle. Fortunately, budgerigars are ready to breed at the age of three months —a necessity for survival; during periods of drought, hundreds of thousands of the parakeets perish. To fend off disaster the birds have developed protective measures. Daily visits to water holes like the one at right are routine, but predators such as kites, falcons and dingoes await the budgies' arrival. To confuse their enemies, the birds whirl and circle around the water hole so rapidly that it is almost impossible for predators to pick off a victim.

118

The gaudy birds at left (above), with their violet-blue heads, red-orange breasts, blue bellies, green beaks and orange eyes, are deservedly known as rainbow lories. Found in the wet forest areas of Australia, they travel in flocks sometimes numbering well over 100. They are not only the most colorful but also the noisiest of the Australian parrots, screeching at the top of their lungs from morning to night.

In sharp contrast to the rainbow lory, the tiny fig parrot (left, below) is quiet and reserved. It lives high in the thickest branches of fig trees, and its dark plumage makes it difficult to spot. As many as 200 fig parrots have taken up residence in a single tree, their presence betrayed only by falling drops of fig juice.

Down Under Exotics

Though parrots inhabit all the warmer regions of the world, Australia not only harbors some of the most colorful and exotic members of the family but it is also believed to be the original homeland of parrots. Of the world total of 315 species, 55 inhabit Australia and approximately 146 occur in New Guinea, New Zealand and neighboring islands. Outstanding among Down Under parrots is the elegant red-winged parrot of Australia (above), one of the most spectacular of the island continent's bird population.

Parrots are commonly divided into two main groups: the parrots and cockatoos, which have blunt tongues and feed on grass and fruits, and the brush-tongued lories, which subsist on the nectar and pollen of the flowers. All parrots have the unmistakable crooked profile of the family and unusual feet with two toes pointing forward and two backward. With the exception of two species—keas and kakas—parrots are monogamous, mating for life. Most are hole-nesters, most frequently using tree cavities but sometimes burrowing in the ground. Brooding takes from 18 to 30 days and in the majority of species is left to the female, although both parents share the chore of feeding their raucous, naked young.

Bird Aristocrats

The beauties on these pages represent three different families of birds. But all share certain attributes—imposing size, erect posture and regal stateliness—that mark them as true aristocrats of the bird kingdom.

The white-plumaged grande dame opposite, examining her nest while a young bird stands respectfully aside, is appropriately named the royal spoonbill. Winging all across Australia except in desert regions, the 30-inch-long spoonbill builds its nest on marsh plants or broken reeds and lays its eggs, which rarely number more than five, in the early spring. The pink-legged wader below, boasting an outsize black bill and a height of 51 inches from the tip of its bill to its toes, is the jabiru, Australia's only stork. The jabiru is most often seen in or near the water. The Cape Barren goose at right is unique to Australia, as are the elegant black swans shown overleaf. The swans range widely, but the goose is confined to offshore islands from Cape Leeuwin in the west to New South Wales in the east.

Credits

Cover—F. Prenzel, Bruce Coleman, Inc. 1—H.&J. Beste. 5—G.E. Schmida, B.C., Inc. 6–7—K. Tanaka, Animals Animals. 9—Dr. G. Gerster, Rapho, Photo Researchers, Inc. 13, 14–15—H. Gritscher, Animals Animals. 16–17—Dr. G. Gerster, Rapho, P.R., Inc. 19—H.&J. Beste. 20—H.&J. Beste, Tom Stack & Assoc. 21 (top)—H.&J. Beste; (bottom)—Bruce Coleman, Inc. 22–23—P.R., Inc. 23—J. Carnemolla, Scoopix. 24 (left)—J. Brownlie, B.C., Inc.; (right)—J. Dominis, Time Inc. 25 (top and bottom)—J. Dominis, Time Inc. 27—F. Erize, B.C., Ltd. 28—J. Dominis, Time Inc. 29 (left)—G. Schmida, B.C., Inc.; (right)—H.&J. Beste. 30 (left and right)—J. Dominis, Time Inc. 31 (top left and right)—J. Dominis, Time Inc.; (bottom)—H.&J. Beste. 32–33—K. Tanaka, Animals Animals. 35—Nina Leen. 36–37—G. Lewis, Scoopix. 38—J. Dominis, Time Inc. 38–39—W. Garst, Tom Stack Assoc. 41—J. Dominis, Time Inc. 42—K. Tanaka, Animals Animals. 43—J. Dominis, Time Inc. 44–45—J. Fields, P.R., Inc. 45—H.&J. Beste. 46—J. Dominis, Time Inc. 47—Bruce Coleman, B.C., Ltd. 48—H.&J. Beste, Tom Stack Assoc. 49—H.&J. Beste. 50—M. Morcombe, Scoopix. 52—T. McHugh, Melbourne Zoo, P.R., Inc. 52–53—J. Dominis, Time Inc. 55—H.&J. Beste. 56–57—T. McHugh, Taronga Zoo, P.R., Inc. 56—G. Pizzey, B.C., Ltd. 57—D. Baglin, Animals Animals. H.&J. Beste, Tom Stack & Assoc. 60—G. Pizzey, B.C., Ltd. 60–61—J. Dominis, Time Inc. 62–63—W. Garst, Tom Stack & Assoc., 63—J. Dominis, Time Inc. 64 (top)—D. Clyne, Scoopix; (bottom)—G. Lewis, Scoopix. 65—H.&J. Beste. 66 (top)—H.&J. Beste. 66–67—J. Dominis, Time Inc. 67–71—H.&J. Beste. 72–73—R.R. Pawlowski, B.C., Inc. 75—L. Riley, B.C., Inc. 77—R.&D. Keller, Scoopix. 78–79—W. Garst, Tom Stack Assoc. 79—D. Roff. 81—H.&J. Beste. 82—J. Dominis, Time Inc. 83 (top)—Bruce Coleman, Ltd.; (bottom)—A.B. Joyce, P.R., Inc. 84—D. Baglin, Animals Animals. 85—W. Garst, Tom Stack Assoc. 89—H.&J. Beste. 90–91—G.E. Schmida, B.C., Inc. 91—K. Tanaka, Animals Animals. 96—G.E. Schmida, B.C., Inc. 97 (top, left)—H.&J. Beste; (bottom, left)—G.E. Schmida, B.C., Inc., (top, right)—D. Clyne, Scoopix; (bottom, right)—D. Roff. 98—A.B. Joyce, P.R., Inc. 98–99—H.&J. Beste. 100—J. Carnemolla, Scoopix. 101—T. McHugh, Australian Reptile Park, P.R., Inc. 102—H.&J. Beste. 103—G. Schmida, B.C., Inc. 109—L. Burrows, Time Inc. 110—H.&J. Beste. 111 (top)—R.&D. Keller, Scoopix; (bottom)—J. Carnemolla, Scoopix. 114 (top, left)—R.&D. Keller, Scoopix; (bottom, left)—H.&J. Beste; (right)—H.&J. Beste, Tom Stack Assoc. 115 (top, left)—T.&P. Gardner, Scoopix; (top, right)—H.&J. Beste; (bottom)—R.&D. Keller, Scoopix. 116 (top)—H.&J. Beste; (bottom)—H.&J. Beste, Tom Stack & Assoc. 117—T.&P. Gardner, Scoopix. 118—J. Carnemolla, Scoopix. 119—Bruce Coleman, Ltd. 120 (top)—G. Pizzey, Bruce Coleman, Ltd; (bottom)—H.&J. Beste. 120–121—H.&J. Beste. 122—K. Tanaka, Animals Animals. 123 (top)—T. Vanderschmidt, Animals Animals; (bottom)—H.&J. Beste. 124–125—H. Gritscher, Animals Animals.

Photographs on endpapers are used courtesy of Time-Life Picture Agency, Russ Kinne and Stephen Dalton of Photo Researchers, Inc. and Nina Leen.

Film sequence on page 8 is from "The Loners," a program in the Time-Life Television series Wild, Wild World of Animals.

MAP on pages 10–11 is by Nicholas Fasciano.

ILLUSTRATION on pages 86–87 is by Barbara Will, those on pages 92–95 are by André Durenceau, those on pages 104–107 are by John Groth, and the illustration on page 113 is by Charles Robinson.

Bibliography

Barrett, Charles, An Australian Animal Book. Oxford University Press. 1955.

Beatty, Bill, Unique to Australia. Angus and Robertson, 1962.

Bergamini, David, and the Editors of Time-Life Books, The Land and Wildlife of Australia. Time-Life Books, 1974.

Breeden, Stanley and Kay, Wildlife of Eastern Australia. Collins, 1973.

Chisholm, Alexander H., Bird Wonders of Australia. Michigan State University Press, 1959.

——— ed., Australian Encyclopaedia. The Grolier Society of Australia, 1965.

——— ed., Land of Wonder. Angus and Robertson, 1965.

Cogger, Harold G., Reptiles and Amphibians of Australia. A.H. and A.W. Reed, 1976.

Fleay, David, Nightwatchmen of Bush and Plain. Jacaranda Press, 1968.

Frith, H.J., The Malle-fowl. Angus and Robertson, 1962.

———, and Calaby, J.H., Kangaroo. Humanities Press, 1969.

Frauca, Harry, Australian Bird Wonders. Rigby Ltd., 1974.

Grzimek, Bernhard, Four-legged Australians. Hill and Wang, 1967.

Hill, Robin, Australian Birds. Thomas Nelson, 1967.

Huxley, Elspeth, Their Shining Eldorado. Morrow, 1967.

Kinghorn, J.R., The Snakes of Australia. Michigan State University Press, 1957.

Lyne, Gordon, Marsupials and Monotremes of Australia. Angus and Robertson, 1967.

Marlow, Basil, Marsupials of Australia. Jacaranda Press, 1962.

McMichael, D.F., A Treasury of Australian Wildlife. Ure Smith, 1968.

Moffitt, Ian, and the Editors of Time-Life Books, The Australian Outback. Time-Life International, 1976.

Monkman, Noel, From Queensland to the Great Barrier Reef. Doubleday, 1958.

Morcombe, Michael, Australian Marsupials and Other Native Animals. Scribners, 1974.

———, An Illustrated Encyclopedia of Australian Wildlife. Doubleday, 1974.

Pizzey, Graham, Animals and Birds of Australia. Cassell Australia Ltd., 1966.

Ride, W.D.L., A Guide to Native Mammals of Australia. Oxford University Press, 1970.

Serventy, Vincent, Wildlife of Australia. Thomas Nelson, 1968.

Troughton, Ellis, Furred Animals of Australia. Angus and Robertson, 1941.

Walker, Ernest P., Mammals of the World, Vols. 1 and 2. Johns Hopkins, 1975.

Index